Faustina the Younger

Coinage, Portraits, and Public Image

Martin Beckmann

Numismatic Studies

43

AMERICAN NUMISMATIC SOCIETY

NEW YORK

2021

© 2021 American Numismatic Society

ISBN (hardcover) 978-0-89722-366-9
ISBN (paperback) 978-0-89722-735-3
ISBN (ebook) 978-0-89722-731-5
ISSN 0517-404X

Library of Congress Cataloging-in-Publication Data

Names: Beckmann, Martin, author.
Title: Faustina the Younger : coinage, portraits, and public image / Martin
    Beckmann.
Description: New York : American Numismatic Society, 2021. | Series:
    Numismatic studies, 0517-404X ; 43 | Includes bibliographical references
    and index. | Summary: "The Roman empress Faustina the Younger, wife of
    the emperor Marcus Aurelius and mother to at least eleven imperial
    children, including the future emperor Commodus, not only played a key
    role in Roman history of the 2nd century AD but also was the subject of
    almost unparalleled commemoration in visual media, especially sculpture
    and coinage. This book examines the single largest surviving ancient
    source for the portraiture and public image of Faustina the Younger: the
    coinage struck in her name under Antoninus Pius and Marcus Aurelius. The
    coinage of Faustina the Younger is rich in original iconography and long
    in duration but its chronology and the relationships between its various
    types remain unclear. This study seeks to remedy this situation by
    employing the methodology of die analysis to create a new and firm
    chronology for Faustina's coinage. The results make it possible to
    establish an authoritative typology for Faustina's portraiture and to
    show the precise relationship between the diverse obverse and reverse
    types. The die analysis also clarifies Faustina's complicated
    iconographic program, making it possible to compare it directly with the
    iconography of the coinage of her male contemporaries, which can be
    dated to specific years by imperial titulature. Taken together, these
    results permit a complete re-evaluation of the coinage, portraits and
    public image of Faustina the Younger"-- Provided by publisher.
Identifiers: LCCN 2021004455 (print) | LCCN 2021004456 (ebook) | ISBN
    9780897223669 (cloth) | ISBN 9780897227353 (paper) | ISBN 9780897227315
    (ebook)
Subjects: LCSH: Coinage--Rome--History. | Faustina, Annia Galeria, Empress,
    consort of Marcus Aurelius, Emperor of Rome, -175--Portraits. |
    Faustina, Annia Galeria, Empress, consort of Marcus Aurelius, Emperor of
    Rome, -175--Numismatics. | Coins, Roman. | Rome--Antiquities.
Classification: LCC CJ1003 .B433 2021 (print) | LCC CJ1003 (ebook) | DDC
    737.4932--dc23
LC record available at https://lccn.loc.gov/2021004455
LC ebook record available at https://lccn.loc.gov/2021004456

Cover image: Gold *aureus* of Antoninus Pius (AD 145–161). ANS 1956.184.56.
American Numismatic Society © 2021

To H.M.N.

ACKNOWLEDGEMENTS

Many people helped me during the long process of research and writing. I would like to thank the late Ted Buttrey, who kindly welcomed me at Cambridge in the early stages of data gathering. For the opportunity to present and discuss my early results I am especially indebted to the organizers and attendees of two important colloquia, "Sculpture and Coins" at Harvard in 2011 and "Art in the Round" at Tübingen in 2012, and particularly to Carmen Arnold-Biucchi, Annette Alexandridis, Barbara Borg, Bill Metcalf, Nathan Elkins, and Stefan Krmnicek. For help and discussion at various stages of this project I am grateful to Richard Abdy, Aleksander Bursche, Curtis Clay, Jens-Arne Dickmann, Brad Edwards, Klaus Fittschen, Amanda Hardman, Johan van Heesch, Bettina Kruezer, Ralf von den Hoff, Ute Wartenberg, and Bernhard Weisser. Last but by no means least I thank Andrew Reinhard and the two anonymous reviewers of this manuscript, whose extensive comments led to much improvement of the final draft.

Contents

Introduction

Faustina the Younger:
Coinage, Portraits, and Public Image

ABSTRACT

The Roman empress Faustina the Younger, wife of the emperor Marcus Aurelius and mother to at least eleven imperial children, including the future emperor Commodus, not only played a key role in Roman history of the second century AD but was also, during her lifetime, the subject of almost unparalleled commemoration in visual media, especially sculpture and coinage. This book examines the single largest surviving ancient source for the portraiture and public image of Faustina the Younger: the coinage struck in her name under Antoninus Pius and Marcus Aurelius. The coinage of Faustina the Younger is rich in original iconography and long in duration, but its chronology and the relationships between its various types remain unclear. This study seeks to remedy this situation by employing the methodology of die analysis to create a new and firm chronology for Faustina's coinage. The results make it possible to establish an authoritative typology for Faustina's portraiture and to show the precise relationship between the diverse obverse and reverse types. The die analysis also clarifies Faustina's complicated iconographic program, making it possible to compare it directly with the iconography of the coinage of her male contemporaries, which can be dated to specific years by imperial titulature. Taken together, these results permit a complete re-evaluation of the coinage, portraits, and public image of Faustina the Younger.

INTRODUCTION

Faustina the Younger (AD 130–176) was the daughter of Antoninus Pius and Faustina the Elder. Her mother died in 140, when Faustina was just ten years old; her two brothers and one sister were by then already dead, leaving Faustina as the only surviving child of Pius. Five years later she married Marcus Aurelius, who was almost ten years her senior, in a carefully arranged match designed to perpetuate the imperial dynasty. From this point of view it was a success. Children followed quickly, with a total of at least eleven born over the following fifteen years. Faustina survived the dangers of these multiple childbirths and lived to the age of 46, when she died in the Taurus Mountains of southeastern Turkey, while travelling with her husband. Her last child had been born perhaps six years previously, and she had recently been hailed with a remarkable new title, *Mater Castrorum*, "Mother of the Camp." An unprecedentedly large and long issue of coinage in her name and numerous sculpted portraits (second in number only to those of Livia among imperial women) show that Faustina the Younger had a substantial public presence, presumably connected to the important role she played in the imperial household.

What sort of role was this? Our perception of Faustina's public image has been strongly formed by the main ancient historical sources, especially Cassius Dio and the unknown author of the *Historia Augusta*, which are extremely hostile to her. They accuse Faustina of wonton infidelity and even plotting to overthrow Marcus as emperor. These written accounts have dominated the formation of the historical image of Faustina for centuries. The eighteenth-century English historian Edward Gibbon characterized her thus: "Faustina, the daughter of Pius and the wife of Marcus, has been as much celebrated for her gallantries as for her beauty. The grave simplicity of the philosopher was ill-calculated to engage her wanton levity. [...] Marcus was the only man in the empire who seemed ignorant or insensible of the irregularities of Faustina."[1] Even when he adduced the much more positive evidence of the writings of Marcus himself, Gibbon felt compelled to return to the viewpoint of the slanderers and speculate how it was that the emperor had been so deluded: "In his Meditations, he thanks the gods, who had bestowed on him a wife, so faithful, so gentle, and of such a wonderful simplicity of manners. [... T]he world has laughed at the credulity of Marcus, but Madam Dacier assures us (and we may credit a lady), that the husband will always be deceived, if the wife condescends to dissemble."[2] This view of Faustina persisted at least into the 1930s, when J. Wight Duff wrote in the first edition of volume XI of the *Cambridge Ancient History*, ostensibly discussing the deification of imperial family members, that "the fashion of deifying the women of the Caesars increased, until we find Marcus Aurelius, when his empress Faustina died in Asia Minor, asking the Senate to decree to her divine honours and a memorial temple, while his eulogy implied ignorance, real or simulated, of her notorious depravity."[3] This negative, even hostile reception of Faustina as a historical figure is based on the "evidence" of the main historical sources, all of which post-date Faustina's lifetime, and this is a major problem. Scholars following such an approach have been inspired to explain all other evidence in light of the very negative historical commentary, rather than using these other sources to re-evaluate or critique the historians. This study dispenses entirely with these dubious records until the end, when we can return to them to evaluate their contents from a viewpoint grounded in sources contemporary to Faustina herself.

1. Gibbon 1776, 108.
2. Gibbon 1776, 108–109 and n. 4.
3. Duff 1936, 745–746. He cites *SHA Marc.* 26 and Cass. Dio 72.31.

Coinage is the most important of the contemporary evidence. Faustina's image appeared on a large portion of the imperial coinage struck during the reigns of her father (Pius) and her husband (Marcus). The number of coins bearing her name found in a very large hoard (about eighty thousand coins total) of Roman silver *denarii* at Reka Devnia, Bulgaria, in 1929 give some impression of how prominent Faustina was in the coinage of the period. Antoninus Pius is represented by 6,619 *denarii*; his (deceased) wife Faustina the Elder by 3,557; his adopted son Marcus Aurelius by 6,596; while Faustina the Younger's portrait appears on 2,989.[4] Roughly speaking, for every two *denarii* produced at this time bearing the image of an emperor, one was issued with the image of an empress. Faustina's coinage is further marked out by the fact that from the very beginning, while she was still a teenager, she bears the name Augusta while her husband Marcus is still called Caesar (rather than Augustus).[5] One of the most striking aspects of her coinage is the great variety of its obverse portraiture, with frequent dramatic changes being made to the empress's appearance throughout her reign. The reverses similarly depicted a diversity of images: goddesses, personifications, even children which have often been interpreted as Faustina's own, accompanied by inscriptions proclaiming to the public the virtues associated with the empress. The mint where these coins were produced was located in Rome, as close to the center of power as it was possible to get, and its staff of freedmen and slaves were members of the imperial household itself. A vast and highly varied provincial coinage also existed, mainly bronze coins struck by individual cities in the east; this material is beyond the scope of the present study.[6]

Normally, Roman imperial coinage may be dated—sometimes with a good deal of precision—by the changing titles of the emperors. Coins of both Antoninus Pius and Marcus Aurelius, for example, are usually datable to within a single year because they are marked with the annual iterations of the tribunician power. Coins of imperial women, on the other hand, present much greater difficulties. Faustina is called "Faustina Augusta" from the beginning of coinage in her name. The only chronological indicator appears to be the presence or absence of filiation ("daughter of Antoninus Pius"), which is present on her earliest coinage and is thought to have disappeared when Pius died. But, as will be seen, even this is not certain. The methodology used to solve this problem is die analysis, described in detail in Chapter 1. It allows the precise sequence not only of portraits and reverse types but also of the individual dies used to strike the coins to be established. This is a powerful aid in determining the chronology of Faustina's coinage and of the portraits, images and inscriptions it bears.

Obtaining a solid chronology is only part of the solution to the problem of understanding Faustina's coinage. The second step is the interpretation of the images on the coins after a correct sequence and clear interrelationship of types has been established. What was the purpose of these images? Who chose them? To what end? What can we learn from them? I approach this problem of interpretation from two angles. The first is to use the information provided by the die analysis to evaluate earlier theories and interpretations of Faustina's

---

4. These counts are the total number of *denarii* for each ruler in the Sofia holdings only. Mouchmov 1934, 5.

5. On Augusta and imperial women, see Levick 2014, 34–36.

6. For an impression of how the provincial coinage related to the central Roman coinage in the case of Faustina the Elder, see Beckmann 2012, 73–83. Faustina the Younger was much more prevalent on the coinage of the provinces than was her mother.

coinage. This can be particularly illuminating from a methodological point of view, since it offers the potential to show whether an interpretation based on a certain theory arrived at the correct answer, or not. The second angle is to present a number of new interpretations based on the patterns revealed by the die analysis and on the limited ancient evidence we have as to how coin images were chosen, why, and for what purpose.

The difficulty of interpretation of numismatic images, already substantial, is complicated when problems and methodologies from neighboring disciplines are brought into the mix. In the case of Faustina the Younger this is most evident in the problem of her portraiture. The study of Roman portraiture, focused primarily on sculpted three-dimensional heads, has developed its own particular methodology, one that incorporates the evidence of coins but does not prioritize it. Most importantly the field of portrait studies has developed its own taxonomic approach to the material it studies. The basic units of portrait classification are called types, of which any given emperor normally has more than one. Each type comprises a group of portraits, called replicas, of which the members share specific formalistic traits, especially details of hair arrangement. The field of portrait studies also has its own interpretive theory. Types are normally considered creations occasioned by special events such as triumphs or anniversaries. Thus to portrait scholars a portrait type has a meaning beyond its use to identify its subject; it is historically, perhaps even ideologically, significant. This theory has recently seen some challenges but it remains dominant in the field (see Chapter 5). In the case of Faustina the theory of portrait types is particularly relevant, since Klaus Fittschen proposed in 1982 that each of her many portraits was created to mark the birth of a child. This theory has been much debated (see Chapter 7) but until now it has not been possible to objectively test it. Die analysis of the numismatic evidence makes such a test possible, by revealing clearly the exact development of the iconography of the coinage, both portraits and reverse types, and making its chronology clear. In addition to testing Fittschen's theory, this analysis also presents the opportunity to create a much more nuanced and detailed history of Faustina's numismatic iconography, including portraiture and, by extension, to critique some of the established methodologies of portrait studies in general.

The organization of this material presents a major problem. On the one hand, there are a number of major, specific questions that need to be explored: the chronology of Faustina's coinage; the exact nature and sequence of Faustina's portraiture; the role of portraiture in the construction of Faustina's public image; the validity of traditional approaches to portrait study. These themes call for individual treatment and focused attention. But at the same time the evidence of the coins, arranged in the newly-won sequence revealed by die analysis, presents a narrative that begs to be followed, a timeline along which we can observe the connections between various media and iconographic elements. I have chosen a compromise approach designed to highlight the most important aspects of both individual research questions and of the overall narrative of the numismatic iconography. After an introduction to the materials and method, three chapters trace the chronological development of Faustina's coinage, where possible setting the iconography in the context of contemporary history as well as the contemporary coinage of Antoninus Pius and Marcus Aurelius. The next three chapters are devoted to Faustina's portraiture, first to the discussion of the issues and theories involved in portrait study generally and the history of the study of her portraits specifically, then an analysis of the typology and chronology of Faustina's portraits as revealed by the die links, and finally a consideration of the message of her portraiture including, but not limited to, an evaluation of Fittschen's theory. In the conclusion I consider Faustina's overall public image, which originally the product of a number of display and communication media of which we have only partial knowledge. Here I contextualize the later, hostile written records in light of what is revealed by contemporary evidence. What emerges is still an incomplete picture of Faustina the Younger, but it is hoped a clearer one, one stripped of the misleading baggage of dubious source material. The results will also hopefully provide a starting point for further analysis of the coinage and public image of this empress.

Chapter 1

Material and Methodology

The Roman empire of the second century AD used a somewhat complex system of coinage. It was fundamentally based on a three-metal system of gold, silver, and copper-alloy (copper, bronze or brass, all of which may be abbreviated AE by numismatists, from the Latin *aes*).[1] There was a major division between east and west. All coinage for the western provinces (including Italy) in all metals was produced in Rome. All gold coinage for the entire empire was also produced in Rome, but the eastern part of the empire used a variety of systems for silver and bronze coinage. Syria, Cappadocia, and western Asia Minor based their silver coinage on various Greek denominations, some produced locally and some produced in Rome. For small change, however, dozens of individual cities relied on their own production of bronze coinage, which was decorated both with imperial portraits and with local gods and objects. And Egypt was a province apart, with its own system of silver and bronze coinage produced locally in Alexandria.

This study is focused on the coinage of Faustina issued in Rome. This coinage was the largest by number produced in the empire, had the widest circulation, and was minted in very close proximity to the center of imperial power—and thus, potentially, to imperial control. It was struck in a variety of denominations, the most important being the gold *aureus*, the silver *denarius* (25 to an *aureus*), and the copper-alloy *sestertius* (a large coin, 4 to a *denarius*), *dupondius* (half a *sestertius*) and *as* (quarter of a *sestertius*). The most common coin in circulation was the *denarius*. In the second century AD all these coins bore the portrait of a member of the imperial family: an emperor or, increasingly as the century progressed, an empress. A handy indicator of the relative proportions of coinage struck in the names of emperors and empresses comes from the very large hoard of about 80,000 *denarii* (weight

---

1. On Roman coinage, see Burnett 1987 and Mattingly 1960.

about 350 kg) found in 1929 at Reka Devnia (ancient Marcianopolis) in Bulgaria.[2] In this hoard, only 0.2% of Trajan's coinage (by coin count) consists of types bearing portraits of the female members of the imperial family. There is a dramatic increase under Hadrian, when about 10% of his coinage (again by count) bears the portrait of his wife Sabina. Under Antoninus Pius this already high ratio jumps again, with the number of coins struck in the names of Faustina the Elder (mostly posthumous) and Faustina the Younger totaling roughly half the number of those of Antoninus Pius and Marcus Aurelius; every third *denarius* issued under these rulers depicted a woman on the obverse.[3] This amounted to a dramatic change in the iconographic makeup of the Roman coinage.

Faustina's coinage is marked with her portrait and an inscription on the obverse, and with a design (most often a goddess or personification) on the reverse. The obverse inscriptions state her official titulature and they change over time; the major division is between inscriptions identifying her as daughter (*filia*, abbreviated as FIL or simply F) of Antoninus Pius, and inscriptions that do not mention this relationship but rather say only "Faustina Augusta." As will be seen, die link evidence indicates that this change (the dropping of *filia* from Faustina's nomenclature) happened shortly before the death of her father Antoninus in 160 (see discussion in Chapter 4). The inscriptions giving Faustina's filiation appear in six varieties, and in this study I have followed the abbreviations used by Harold Mattingly (*BMCRE* IV) to identify them in short form:

fa	FAVSTINAE AVG PII AVG FIL
fb	FAVSTINA AVG PII AVG F (no *aurei* are known with this legend)
fc	FAVSTINA AVG ANTONINI AVG PII FIL
fd	FAVSTINA AVG PII AVG FIL
fe	FAVSTINA AVGVSTA AVG PII F/FIL
ff	FAVSTINA AVGVSTA

Faustina's own appearance likewise changes over time, most notably in her coiffure, but also in subtler transformations to her physiognomy. In keeping with the standard practice among portrait scholars (see Chapter 5), I have grouped Faustina's portraits into Types based primarily on the criterion of hair arrangement. The die analysis indicates that this criterion is valid in most cases, and where it is not (in particular in the development of variants of Type 1), this is made clear by the die links. Types are identified by numbers. Sometimes there are small but significant differences between examples of a single portrait type; these, again following normal practice, are identified as "variants" and identified by a lower-case letter following the type number.[4] So Faustina's numismatic portraiture begins with Type 1,

2. Mouchmov 1934.
3. The numbers in the Sofia museum are: Pius 6,619; Faustina the Elder 3,557; Marcus 6,971; Faustina the Younger 2,989. I cite these figures here as rough guides to the commonness of Faustina's coinage only; on methodological issues in using hoard evidence, see Noreña 2011, 28–36. The Reka Devnia hoard remains by far the single largest such find; its contents alone account for well more than half of the data (148,421 silver coins) assembled by Noreña.
4. In this I follow the practice of Fittschen (1982) in his own study of Faustina's portraits.

but soon Variants 1a and 1b appear. The types, variants and the criteria by which they are distinguished are explained in detail in Chapter 6.

The reverses of Faustina's coinage bear various motifs and inscriptions, the discrete combinations of which are called "types" by numismatists. Some reverse inscriptions merely continue Faustina's titulature, but these are a small minority; most spell out the name of the illustrated goddess, personification or virtue. The relationship between inscription and image thus ranges from obvious (VENVS paired with the image of a woman holding an apple) to obscure (CONCORDIA paired with the image of a bird). The challenge is interpretation. One of the great advantages offered by die analysis is that it allows us to reconstruct the exact iconographic and epigraphic context of the coin types, thus giving us new evidence to assist in their interpretation.

The Meaning and Control of Coin Types

What was the purpose of the images on Roman coins?[5] Their primary function was presumably to guarantee the value of the coin and to make it acceptable as payment, which from the earliest times was accomplished by employing images connected to the issuing state. Thus in the second century BC the Roman coinage, following Greek tradition, was marked with busts of Roma and images of the Dioscuri (on the silver) and Janus and a ship's prow (on the bronze). This changed in the later second century when types related to the family history of the officials responsible for the coinage, the *tresviri monetales*, began to appear on the silver *denarius*. The *tresviri monetales* were a group of three young men, elected yearly and part of a larger group of minor magistrates who were at the very beginning of their senatorial careers; their job was to supervise the production of coinage and, apparently, to determine its types.[6] The "family" types that appeared on the *denarii* bearing their names likely reflected competition among the elite and thus may have functioned as "advertising" for the family involved, though they also recalled great achievements of the Roman state, and in addition probably (and perhaps primarily) served as control-marks, identifying the coins issued by each moneyer and thus assuring his accountability.[7] The coin types produced by the generals and dictators of the late second and first centuries appear to reflect a sharpening of this focus, being based on divinities associated with or honours won by these military strongmen. This process culminated in the imperial period that might properly be seen as beginning with Caesar, who consolidated control over the mint in the hands of his own slaves and whose coinage was the first produced in Italy to bear a portrait of a living Roman leader.[8] The office of the *monetales* remained in place—and the family types of the moneyers even made a brief re-

5. The scholarly literature on the questions of the significance of Roman coin types is large. See e.g., Elkins 2017, 6–12; Noreña 2011, 190–200; Levick 1999; Crawford 1983.

6. On the *tresviri monetales*, see Hamilton 1969.

7. Hamilton (1969, 169) detects a greater number of *monetales* going on to high-profile postions in the post-Sullan period and attributes this to the advantage given by the office in promoting their careers. Sutherland (1986, 88) argues that both the moneyers' names and types "were obligatory elements designed to facilitate the necessary spot-checking of the weight and intrinsic quality of coinage."

8. Suet. *Iul.* 76.3: *Praeterea monetae publicisque vectigalibus peculiares servos praeposuit.* "And in addition he placed his own slaves in charge of the mint and the public revenues."

appearance on coins in the reign of Augustus—but the imagery of the coinage was thereafter dominated by the imperial portrait and by reverse types related to the emperor.[9]

Roman imperial coin types were very often topical. That is to say, images and inscriptions were frequently placed on them that referred directly to contemporary events. A good example is the depiction on coins of Trajan of his new Forum complex on *aurei* that were first issued in January of the year 112.[10] We know from the *Fasti Ostienses* that Trajan dedicated his Forum on January 1 of that year, the same day on which he assumed the office of consul for the sixth time. We also know from die analysis that the very earliest of his coins with the title COS VI also bore depictions of his Forum and of the Basilica Ulpia.[11] This concept of topicality, the possibility that the images and inscriptions on Roman imperial coinage have a direct relation to important contemporary events, is key to the interpretation of the coinage of Faustina. It is important to note that the degree of topicality tended to vary between the coinage metals. Gold and bronze tended to have types more clearly relevant to contemporary events, while silver, which was produced in much greater quantity, tended towards less topical types. The reason, as I have argued elsewhere, is at least partly to do with the substantial time-pressure placed on die engravers to provide sufficient material for the striking of *denarii*.[12] Simpler designs, such as those with single-figures, were easier to engrave than the more complex compositions often associated with topical types. This is not always the case, and there are certainly examples of *denarii* bearing complicated and detailed scenes, but it is generally true.

Who chose the coin types under the empire? In the middle of the second century AD the *monetales* were still in office, but a massive organization had grown up around the monarch; this was the imperial court, or *aula*.[13] The center of power in the court was the *familia Caesaris*, which included not only the emperor and his relatives, but also slaves and freedmen, some of whom held posts of great influence. In addition, a number of powerful new equestrian posts were created and were considered part of the court. Among these was the *a rationibus*, a top-ranking official in charge of finances; subordinate to him was a new post related to the mint: the *procurator monetae*. This latter office is first attested under Trajan, but may have come into being earlier; the responsibilities of the post are not known.[14] Lower-ranking officials, imperial freedmen, administered the mint operations themselves (see below in the discussion of the mint). The implication is that the chain of command now ran from the mint up directly into the imperial court. This situation, combined with the fact that each coin reverse image was paired with an imperial portrait on the obverse, means that the iconography of the imperial coinage was very closely connected to the emperor. These images should be thought of as having been chosen by, if not the emperor himself (though a number of ancient sources say just that), then a high-ranking official who would first obtain imperial assent before ordering

9. A concise summary of the development of the iconography of Roman coinage in this period is provided by Howgego (1995, 67–70); a more detailed discussion is provided by Sutherland 1986.

10. For the coinage of Trajan in 112, see Beckmann 2007.

11. On the early coinage of Trajan dated COS VI, see Beckmann 2000 and 2007.

12. On topicality in Roman coinage and the practical aspects of its production, see Beckmann 2009.

13. On the imperial court, see Wallace-Hadrill 1996.

14. On the *procurator monetae*, see Peachin 1986.

the types to be employed in the mint.[15] The images on coins therefore should be seen as resulting from decisions made at the very heart of the *aula* and thus reflecting content that originated in close proximity to the emperor.[16] Liesbeth Claes has recently adduced evidence for the reign of Nero that indicates the *a rationibus* was at the key decision maker, or at least the key figure who implemented type changes.[17]

Would Faustina herself have had any influence over what was depicted on "her" coinage? There is very little evidence that can help us answer this question. The fact that Faustina's portrait and name occupy the obverse of the coinage does not necessarily mean that she had control of what appeared on the reverse. But the mechanics of type selection were most likely complicated and probably involved decisions made at various levels, from the mint all the way up to the *aula*. That a woman could have influence in the *aula* is suggested by Suetonius's reference to a *libertinam aulicam gratiosam*, "an influential freedwoman of the court," whom Otho professed to love in order to insinuate himself with Nero (in which he succeeded).[18] Even if Suetonius is merely repeating a story for which he has no first-hand evidence, we might assume that he, who himself rose to a very high level in the *aula* early in the reign of Hadrian, at least considered such a situation plausible. We have no evidence of the involvement of imperial women in the various councils that advised the emperor, and there is no suggestion that they interacted in an official capacity with governors, procurators, or other high imperial officials.[19] But we should be aware of opportunities for indirect influence, or of reflections in the medium of coinage of other ways in which Faustina might have exerted her power at court.

Who was the audience for the messages conveyed by the images on the coinage? This public included people who received imperial payment, especially the army but also the urban plebs in the city of Rome. Antoninus Pius gave nine distributions of money to the people of Rome and Marcus Aurelius gave five in the time before Faustina's death. These would have been ideal opportunities for large amounts of freshly minted coin to come into the hands of the Romans. C. H. V. Sutherland argues that another important audience would have been the Senate, and the types on coins would have acted as "a perpetual reminder of where the real power lay."[20]

15. The ancient sources include Cassius Dio (47.25.3), who attributes to Brutus the choice of the coin type with liberty cap and daggers indicating the murder of Caesar, and Suetonius who writes (*Aug.* 94.12) that Augustus ordered the issue of a silver coin marked with his birth-sign and (*Nero* 25.2) that Nero ordered a coin struck with an image of himself as a lyre-player.

16. This is similar to the conclusion reached by Alexandridis (2004), although by different reasoning. Speaking about imperial iconography in general (7): "... ich glaube, daß bestimmte ikonographische Elemente oder Neuerungen im Kaiserbild auf eine Zentrale zurückzuführen sind, die ich mit dem Kaiserhaus und seiner engeren Umgebung gleichsetze," and about coins in particular (9): "Ich gehe im folgenden davon aus, daß die aus der Reichsprägung stammenden Münzen der Frauen des Kaiserhauses als bestdokumentiertes und mehr oder weniger unmittelbares Zeugnis kaiserlicher Selbstdarstellung gelten können."

17. Claes 2014. The evidence involves changes of coin typology at the same time the holder of the office *a rationibus* changed.

18. Suet., *Otho* 2.2 "an influential freedwoman of the court," trans. J. C. Rolfe, Cambridge, MA, 1914. See Alföldy 1985, 108.

19. The closest we come is the mention by Philostratus (*Vit. Soph.* 560) of Faustina and her daughter Vibia's intercession on behalf of the Athenians in a trial involving Herodes Atticus. Levick (2014, 74) notes that the women "are presented as suppliants" in this scene, and one wonders if Philostratus simply made it up.

20. Sutherland 1986, 92.

THE PRACTICALITIES OF THE ROMAN MINT

Since this study is based on detailed examination and reconstruction of coin production, a basic knowledge of the physical structure and operation of the Roman imperial mint will help the reader better understand the methodology and the results. Rather surprisingly we know quite a lot about this. The mint of the imperial period was located southwest of the Colosseum; some of its ruins have (probably) been found, and part of its ground plan appears to have been preserved in a fragment of the Severan marble map of Rome known as the *Forma Urbis*.[21] From this we learn that the mint was a large rectangular building with a series of small rooms of regular size arranged around a central courtyard. These rooms opened only to the courtyard and were presumably workshops in which the coins were struck. Numismatists often use this term, "workshop," interchangeably with another term, "anvil," to designate an individual coin production site where a single obverse and single reverse die would be in use.

Each of these workshops would be staffed by a group of specialized workers, about whom we have some surprisingly precise information. This is in the form of three inscriptions discovered on the site of the mint in the sixteenth century.[22] Dated to the reign of Trajan, they tell us that the mint was under the command of an imperial freedman named Felix, *optio et exactor auri argenti aeris*, "officer and superintendent of gold, silver, and bronze." The staff consisted of 89 men, some freedmen and some slaves, who appear to have been divided into sixteen groups, each headed by a man called an *officinator* (=person in charge of an *officina*, or workshop). Each workshop had of a *signator* (man who held the upper die and who thus put the design—*signum*—on the coin), a *suppostor* (man who put the coin blank under the upper die), and three *malliatores* (hammer-men, the most physically demanding job in the mint, and thus the reason for assigning three to each workshop). Although there are sixteen *officinatores* and *signatores*, there are only ten blank-placers, suggesting that the number of workshops in production could vary over time. Just as in the army, illness and injury presumably resulted in a constant fluctuation of strength in the mint's workforce.

The main implication of this information, or at least the one most important for the purpose of this study, is that the Roman mint was a large-scale operation where coins would have been produced in multiple workshops simultaneously. The maximum number of workshops was, perhaps, more than ten and less than twenty (though it is not impossible that sixteen, the number given in the Trajanic inscriptions, was the standard number). The exact number actually in use at any one time would have been determined by how many coins of what denomination the mint was required to produce. The highest volume component of the coinage was the silver *denarius*, so we might imagine a majority of workshops dedicated to producing these. The remaining workshops would produce gold and bronze coinage. The proportions probably changed over time, depending on need and on the supply of metal available. Exactly this sort of change over time is visible in the die links of Faustina's gold coinage, where sometimes only one workshop is attested, while at other times two parallel workshops are indicated. The key point here is that the die links themselves provide the clues

21. *LTUR* III, s.v. "Moneta, M. Caesaris (Reg. III)" (F. Coarelli).
22. *CIL* 6.42–44 = *ILS* 1633–1635. For discussion, see Woytek 2012.

Figure 1.1. *Aureus* of Faustina showing Venus with a staff and globe (**VB4/fd2**; ANS 1997.122.1). 18 mm. Scale 2:1.

Figure 1.2. *Aureus* of Faustina showing a bird (**CB17/fd2**; ANS 1997.122.2). 19.5 mm. Scale 2:1.

from which we may deduce the sequence and organization of die use, and thus obtain a glimpse of how the mint functioned in actual practice.

Methodology: Die Analysis

The methodology used to create this new chronology for the coinage of Faustina the Younger is die analysis (often also called die study). Die analysis seeks to reconstruct, as far as possible, the exact sequence of use of dies in the mint. Dies are the metal punches, engraved at one end with a design, that were used to strike ancient coins. These (as best we can tell from a few preserved examples) were in the form of iron bars or rods, one (the obverse die, usually bearing the "head") set into a firm support (normally called an "anvil"), the other (the reverse die) held in the hand. In the process of minting, a metal blank was placed on the upper surface of the obverse die, then the reverse die was placed on top of it and struck with a hammer. These hand-engraved (and therefore unique) dies left their impressions on the coins they were used to strike, and thus the dies can be identified by studying the coins they produced.[23] Initially developed in the nineteenth century, the method was first used to study the products of the early United States mint, but was soon applied with great success to undated Greek coin issues; it has been less often applied to Roman coinage.[24] Part of the reason is that the volume

23. On ancient minting practice, see Grierson 1975, 100–111.
24. Metcalf 1996, 253.

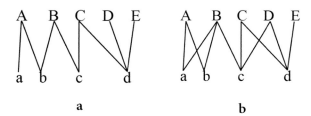

Figure 1.3. A theoretical representation of a simple die link chain (a.). A die link chain representing the simultaneous use of more than one reverse and obverse die (b.).

of surviving material has been thought too large for such a study to succeed.[25] But over the last half-century a series of die studies of Roman coinage have shown that this pessimistic appraisal was incorrect, and that good results may be obtained for many different issues and denominations.[26]

The success of the method depends on how dies were made and employed. To produce the millions of coins required by the Roman state, hundreds, even thousands of dies were cut, because eventually each would wear out or break under the blow of a hammer. All these dies were not cut at once, but rather individually as needed or in small groups. Presumably the material of worn or broken dies was recycled as part of this process. Naturally the obverse and reverse dies would not wear out or break at exactly the same time, so it would be necessary to create a replacement for one die, which would then be used together with the die that was still good. This would create a "link" between the old (worn or broken) die and its newly cut replacement through their common use of the still-good, unreplaced die. For example, compare Figs. 1.1 and 1.2. Both coins were struck using different reverse dies; in fact, they have entirely different reverse types. But the details of the obverse are exactly the same on each coin. We can then say that there is a die link between these two different reverse dies, showing that they were in use in the mint at about the same time. This also shows that these two different reverse types were contemporary.

The process of die replacement, if carried on over time in a series of continuous production, leaves evidence of the sequence of die use in the form of these links. If enough links can be found, it is theoretically possible to recreate the entire sequence of die use in a mint.

In actual practice the identification of dies is normally not difficult, but it is time consuming. One begins by selecting a coin from the group to be analyzed; its obverse and reverse dies are designated the first of their relevant series. Images of these "dies" (actually of the coin struck by the dies) are placed in a file and the first entry is made in the die catalogue. Then the second coin is selected and it is compared with these die images. If differences in detail reveal it to have been struck by different dies, an independent entry is made in the catalogue and images of these new dies are added to the die files. If, however, it proves to have been struck

25. E.g., Strack (1933, 2) on the "impossibility" of clarifying the chronology of Hadrian's coinage by die analysis: "Bei der erstaunlichen Menge, in der uns die Reichsprägung zur Zeit Hadrians erhalten blieb, wird es immer unmöglich sein, das weite Material nach den einzelnen Stempeln zu ordnen."

26. A summary of the most significant applications of die study to Roman coinage up to the 1980s is given by Metcalf (1996). See also Duncan-Jones (1994, 150–161) (studies of selected second century AD coinage with an eye to determining volume of coin production); Beckmann 2007 and 2012 (chronological studies of the coinage of Trajan and Faustina I).

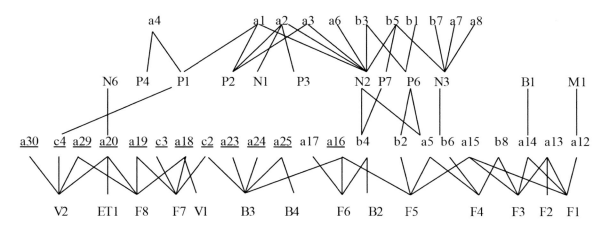

Figure 1.4. An actual die link chart representing minting of *aurei* under Trajan, AD 112.

by the same die or dies (highly unlikely at this early stage of analysis!) a sub-entry is made in the catalogue under the already-identified die. With well-struck and well-preserved coins (as most *aurei* are), the comparison is relatively easy and there is almost never any doubt or uncertainty about die identifications. In the rare cases that doubt has arisen, I have split rather than lumped any uncertain dies. That is to say: if two coins appear to have been struck by the same die but for whatever reason, perhaps because of a poor photograph, I could not be certain, I have created two distinct die identities. This situation however is extremely rare.

When the die analysis is complete, a die chart can be drawn up by meticulously drafting the links between dies as documented in the catalogue.[27] Normally this requires multiple drafts before the best arrangement (the one where there is a minimum of crossed links) is found. The simplest possible pattern of links would be as indicated in Fig. 1.3a (where a, b, etc. indicate obverse dies, and A, B, etc. indicate reverse dies, and the lines indicate links between the dies). This diagram would represent a situation where only one pair of dies existed at a time, and where each worn die was immediately replaced by a new one. The situation of course can be, and normally is, more complicated. If, for example, more than one reverse and/ or obverse die was cut at a time, and these two reverse dies were used interchangeably, e.g., on different days over their lifespan, a series of links like those in Figure 1.3b might result. The crossed link-lines indicate that some obverse dies were used with more than one reverse die, and vice-versa.

The situation can become yet more complicated in a large mint like that of imperial Rome. The Roman mint would have been striking coinage in gold, silver, and copper-alloy, probably in a more or less continuous production, in multiple workshops. Numerous obverse dies could be employed at one time, even for single metals; this situation is usually referred to by numismatists as the use of multiple workshops (sometimes using the expression "multiple anvils," after the most fundamental piece of equipment in a workshop), each workshop being defined as a place where one obverse die was in use. From the Trajanic mint-worker

27. For discussion of the theory of die linkage, see Esty 1990.

inscriptions we know that these numbered at least ten. These workshops could have been flexibly employed, assigned to striking different metals in different ratios as required at different times. From earlier die studies it is clear that more than one workshop at a time could be assigned to producing gold coinage. The diagram in Figure 1.4, from a die study of Trajanic *aurei* of AD 112, shows the existence to two parallel workshops.[28] The direction of chronology is from left to right. The underlined obverse dies (e.g., a30) employ a dative case legend, the non-underlined dies (e.g., a4) use a nominative case legend. It can be seen that production was initially split into two workshops, one using dative-case obverses and the other nominative-case obverses. Each workshop also used (almost) exclusively its own set of reverse dies: Nerva (N) and Pater Traianus (P) types were used with the nominative-case obverses, while Forum (F), Basilica (B), and other types were used with dative-case obverses. However, the dative-case obverses were eventually abandoned (for reasons unknown) and the two workshops began to share obverse dies. This example shows above all that the operation and workshop setup of the Roman imperial mint was not rigid, but could change over even short periods of time.

In the gold coinage of Faustina we see evidence of a number of different workshop organizations. At the beginning, in the late 140s, it appears that one workshop was used to produce her *aurei*, using a small stock of dies that was gradually renewed as production proceeded. The result is a single, linear chain of die links. In the late 160s, on the other hand, there is clear evidence of the existence of two workshops operating in parallel to produce gold coinage for Faustina. This is seen in two side-by-side chains, each employing a different portrait type and, for the most part, different reverse types. And in between, in the 150s, there exists a very complicated web of die links that is indicative of production in more than one workshop, with dies shared between them. The implication of all this is that there was no single "normal" organization of production in the mint. Instead, mint organization and workshop use could change over time, presumably depending on the quantity demanded (if more gold needed to be struck, extra workshops could be assigned to its production), or on the control methods employed by the overseers of the operation, or on changes in mint staff. The die link charts allow us to reconstruct, in part at least, the probable system of production used at different times by the mint.

Determining Chronology from Die Links

The die analysis of Faustina's *aurei* employed a data set of 681 coins, assembled from the contents of public collections, published archaeological finds, and trade catalogues. These coins proved to have been struck by 134 obverse and 197 reverse dies. Using Warren Esty's geometric model, the original number of dies can be estimated: 162 obverse and 257 reverse.[29] Thus we can be fairly confident that most of the original number of dies used to strike this coinage are represented in the study, but at the same time it is clear that not all original dies

---

28. From Beckmann 2007, 124, modified.

29. Esty 2006. These are point estimates. The number of singletons for obverse dies is 38, for reverse dies 68. For justification of the validity of the geometric method to estimate original numbers of dies, see Esty 2011.

have been identified. As can be seen from the die link charts, the great majority of these dies link to other dies. Linked dies are described in three broad categories: chains, groups, and pairs. Chains are longer sequences for which an internal chronological order can be determined; these are the key components of the overall numismatic chronology. Groups are shorter sequences of linked dies for which no clear internal chronological order can be determined; they may be as small as three dies. Pairs consist of one obverse and one reverse die that do not link into any larger groups or chains.

The challenges are a) to determine the proper "direction" of each chain (that is, what end is earliest and what end latest), and b) to arrange the chains relative to one another. In die analysis of Greek coinage, the criterion of die wear is often used to accomplish the former; unfortunately die wear is only very rarely observable in the gold coinage of the second century AD: evidently the dies were inspected with care and removed as soon as wear or damage appeared.[30] There are, however, other useful criteria that may be used, the most important of these being the continuation of a legend, portrait, or reverse type from one chain to another. If we have two die chains and at one end of each are coins with the same legends, portraits, and/or reverse types, we may conclude that the two chains should be arranged with these ends in proximity. For example, if one chain begins with legend and type characteristics x and ends with characteristics y, and another chain has at one end characteristics z and at the other y, we should arrange them in sequence as follows:

xxxxxxxxxxxyyy   yyyyyyyyyyzzzzzzzzz

Here, "y" defines the continuing inscription, portrait, and/or type. This approach constitutes the core of the chronology laid out here. Other evidence may be used to add chronological information. The potentially most useful alternative chronological criterion is the identification of parallels between reverse types used on the coinage of Faustina and types used on the dated coinage of Antoninus Pius or Marcus Aurelius. Such parallels are rare, but when they occur, they potentially offer important fixed points in what otherwise is a relative chronology. This is because the coinage of the male members of the imperial family is generally much more easily dated than that of the women. Most useful is the emperor's tribunician power, which means his holding of the *tribunicia potestas*, the power of the old office of plebeian tribune, which gave him (among many other things) the power to veto decrees of the senate. In the second century the emperor held this office permanently, but officially it only lasted for one year and had to be continually renewed; these iterations appear on the coinage in the form TR P I, II, III, etc. For Pius and Marcus, the tribunician power was entered on December 10 of each year and renewed on the same date in the following year. To simplify matters in the text a single year is normally given for coins of these emperors dated in this manner; thus, e.g., for a coin dated in the text to AD 149 the *precise* range is December 10 AD 148 to December 9 AD 149.

30. A notable exception is seen on a small group of gold coins struck to celebrate the marriage of Faustina the Younger and Marcus Aurelius. The single reverse die, depicting the couple, is paired with obverse dies of Marcus Caesar and Diva Faustina (the Elder). On coins where this reverse is paired with obverse dies of Diva Faustina, a die crack is clearly visible. Presumably the die was kept in use in order to produce a certain required number of coins (see Beckmann 2012, 208).

Another piece of supporting evidence for the chronology of Faustina's coinage is the estimate of its volume of production, as expressed in terms of how many dies were normally used per year by the Roman mint to strike gold coinage. The number of dies used can also provide a rough indication of chronology when compared to the average annual rate of die usage in the Roman mint. This requires the assumption that die use was relatively constant (rather than in fits and starts), but this is in fact suggested by the existence of linear die-linked chains. The rate of die use may be estimated using data from other die studies. In Trajan's reign, between January AD 112 and mid-113 the mint employed 42 obverse dies for the striking of gold coinage, or about 2 per month.[31] Richard Duncan-Jones has utilized die study and statistical formulae to calculate that between 25 and 50 obverse dies were used per year to strike gold coinage in the reign of Hadrian.[32] About 150 obverse dies were employed for the gold coinage produced in the name of Diva Faustina over a period of about 20 years, or about one die every two months, at a time when the mint was also producing gold coinage in the name of Pius and, later, Marcus Caesar and Faustina the Younger.[33] Using this information it is sometimes possible to make rough estimates of dates when the chain of links is sufficiently intact and when there are some trustworthy chronological fixed points present. But because of the unknown variables I make only limited use of this evidence.

FAUSTINA'S CHILDREN

Another important, though problematic, chronological criterion is the date of birth of Faustina's children. The evidence for their birth dates has been discussed by Fittschen, Walter Ameling (in response to Fittschen) and Anthony Birley.[34] Fittschen proposed that 13 children were born, Birley 14, but Ameling more conservatively suggests a total of 11; I follow his reasoning in this study (Ameling discounts two births proposed by Fittschen, for which there is no concrete evidence, and Levick supports this decision; for a more detailed review of the ancient evidence for these children, see Appendix 1).[35] The 11 firmly known children of Faustina are listed below; I have abbreviated their names:[36]

1. Domitia Faustina (November 30, 147)
2. Lucilla (March 7, ca. 149)
3. Annia Faustina (150 or 151?)
4. Titus Antoninus (152?)
5. Titus Aurelius (? name uncertain; ca. 158, died early)
6. Fadilla (159; outlived Commodus)

31. See Beckmann 2007.
32. Duncan-Jones 1994, 150–162.
33. See Beckmann 2012.
34. Fittschen 1982; Ameling 1992; Birley 1987, Appendix 2, stemma F.
35. Fittschen (1982, 23–25) argues on the basis of coins of Pius showing two cornucopiae crowned with child-like heads, that short-lived male twins were born in 149; he also accepts (ibid, 31) the existence of a "Hadrianus" born in the 160s. Levick (2014, 115) calls Ameling's (1992) rejection of the twins of 149 "convincing."
36. Levick (2014, 115–118) provides a fuller list of Faustina's children, with reference to Birley's and Ameling's opinions and to much of the evidence; this is an ideal starting point for anyone interested in the details of the debate.

7. Cornificia (160; lived to 212)
8, 9. **Commodus**, Lucius Antoninus (twins; August 31, 161; Lucius died 4/5 years later)
10. Marcus Verus (ca. 162)
11. Sabina (ca. 170)

Of these, only no. 1 (Domitia, Faustina's first child) and nos. 8 and 9 (the twins Commodus and Lucius Antoninus) are securely dated in year, month and day. For Lucilla (no. 2) we know the day of birth, but must guess the year; here coin evidence is helpful. This study is focused on the numismatic evidence and what it can tell us, rather than how we might associate any given coin types with a supposed birth. Thus I only draw on this information in cases where it appears possible to demonstrate an association between a type or group of types in the die chain and one of these events. Some coin types do clearly refer to births, and the links resulting from the die analysis give powerful evidence that some of these cluster in specific places in the relative chronology. In some cases it is possible to connect such a cluster of birth-themed types with a probable child (or children) but, as the reader will see, by no means all of Faustina's children appear to have been commemorated on the coinage.

Types related to births often stand in apparent contrast to other types in the die link chains. Paul Strack interpreted the alternating cycles of clearly birth-related types (Juno Lucina, Laetitia Publica) with apparently generic types (Venus, Pudicitia) as indication of the death of the child previously celebrated: "After the death of the child, types of general content take their place."[37] But this replacement of a specific birth-focused type by one of more general significance cannot in itself be taken as evidence that the child concerned is dead. More than one child survived Faustina, most famously Commodus but also her second child Lucilla, and these children do not receive continued, running mention on Faustina's coinage. The phenomenon may be better understood if we look at it from the point of view of what can be deduced from observation of type change over time about the normal functioning of type selection in the Roman mint.[38] A historical type, one connected to a specific event, would be struck close to the time of the event that it commemorated. Afterwards, it would drop out of use and be replaced by other types. It was not the continued veracity of the event that dictated its longevity as a type on the coinage, but rather its topicality. That is, if a type was still topical, still directly relevant to a current ongoing situation, it could still be employed; if not, it was likely to be replaced. Thus a type celebrating a birth by showing a swaddled child would necessarily become "out of date" as that child grew.

LITERARY SOURCES

Given the fact that Faustina's image has for hundreds of years been determined by the "information" provided by two main ancient literary sources, the third-century historian Cassius Dio and the anonymous fourth-century author of the imperial biographies generally known as the *Historia Augusta*, it is essential that these sources be examined carefully before

37. Strack 1937, 113. "Nach dem Tode des Kindes treten Typen allgemeineren Inhalts an ihre Stelle."
38. On change of coin types over time and the factors which may have influenced it, see Beckmann 2009.

any of their evidence is accepted. Cassius Dio was a near contemporary to Faustina, having been born in the mid-160s; he was thus about 20 years old when Commodus succeeded Marcus Aurelius. From his own account he was present in Rome when Commodus was emperor, and he appears to have first come to Rome (from Nicaea, his home town) at this time.[39] His accounts of the extravagant excesses of Commodus's reign are presented as powerful eyewitness statements, but we cannot imagine that he had any personal knowledge of the acts or the public profile of Faustina in Rome in her lifetime, since she died before he would have arrived there. The *Historia Augusta* (*HA*) is ostensibly a collection of imperial biographies (beginning with Hadrian) attributed to a number of different authors working between the time of Diocletian and Constantine, but it is in fact the work of a single author writing at the end of the fourth century.[40] He relied heavily on a limited number of late sources, enlivening his accounts where needed by simply making things up. So Timothy Barnes: "The single writer must be imagined much as Dessau and Syme have depicted him—a man with a sense of humour, who often invented things for the sheer fun of romancing, more interested in fiction than in historical truth."[41] In the earlier lives (including those of Pius and Marcus) the *Historia Augusta* does contain much accurate information that can be confirmed from other sources, but fictional insertions are frequent and mostly involve speculation on the character of important people.[42] The most dubious "information" provided by these sources is as follows. Both accuse Faustina of complicity with Avidius Cassius, the governor of Syria who rebelled against Marcus Aurelius in 175. The *Historia Augusta* in addition offers accusations of adultery, including an affair that supposedly yielded the debauched Commodus, and of magic. These stories are suspicious in the extreme and immediately raise fundamental questions. If Faustina was involved in the conspiracy of Avidius, and this was widely known, how could she have survived his downfall? If Faustina had participated in all manner of extramarital affairs, how could the detailed knowledge of these have reached the public while leaving her, again, unaffected?

But we are not totally without better sources (besides the coinage). Most important among these are the writings of her husband Marcus Aurelius, preserved in his so-called *Meditations* and in his correspondence with his tutor Fronto. The letters between Marcus Aurelius and Fronto in particular allow us to catch precious glimpses of the empress and her household. The corpus of Fronto's letters is not a unified work; some were probably published in his lifetime, while others are so brief and unflattering to Fronto (e.g., *Ep., ad M. Caes.* V. 33 and 65, two one-sentence letters consisting entirely of the announcement of a pain in his groin) that it might be imagined that they were published after his death and without his instruction, as Champlin argues.[43] The sole manuscript is also a severe problem, being a double-palimpsest (Fronto written over an earlier text with another text written over Fronto),

39. Millar 1964, 13.
40. On the sources and reliability of the *Historia Augusta*, see Barnes 1978; on its authorship, see most recently Honoré 1987.
41. Barnes 1978, 18.
42. "The high factual content of these *uitae* does not prevent occasional fiction," so Barnes 1978, 47. He gives the example of *Marc.* 8.12–14, an account of the poor character of Lucius Verus.
43. Champlin 1974, 156–157.

whose leaves were subsequently broken up: perhaps three-sevenths of the original text has been lost.[44] Nonetheless, the correspondence of Marcus and Fronto provides a remarkable amount of intimate information about the imperial family between about 139 and Fronto's death in 166. But there are also great gaps: no letters, for instance, to or from either of the Faustinas, even though Fronto's correspondence with Domitia Lucilla, Marcus's birth mother, is included. The reason, suggests Jörg Fündling, was the maintenance of protocol.[45] Such letters may have existed, but it was not proper for Fronto to publish them.[46] In addition to these letters, we have a few words about Faustina from Marcus his *Meditations* (originally titled "To Himself"). In one instance (*Med.* 9.3) Marcus discusses death as a natural process: "Even as you await the baby's emergence from the womb of your wife, so await the hour when the little soul shall glide forth from its sheath."[47] The connection between birth and death would have been especially clear to Marcus and Faustina, who were fated to experience the deaths of a number of their offspring. By focusing exclusively on contemporary sources, we can better form an impression of the nature of Faustina's image was while she was alive, both in public and in private.

The Portraiture of Faustina the Younger

Many portrait heads survive from ancient times (mostly in stone), but it took a surprisingly long time for scholars to learn how to separate the images of members of the imperial family from the others (normally called "private portraits," though some of their subjects had quite public roles). The crucial development was the application of comparisons between labeled portraits (especially those on coins) and unlabeled ones (especially those in three dimensions). As this method was pursued in the nineteenth century, it became clear that imperial portraits exist in distinct versions, for each of which there could be multiple accurate copies. This led to the establishment of what is perhaps the most important concept in Roman portrait studies: that of "type" (see Chapter 5). The different versions within portraits of a single subject are called types, and they are most often distinguished by distinctive arrangements of the hair. The reproduction of such elements is normally very accurate, indicating that the Romans employed a careful system when creating these copies, and that great attention was paid to details.

Types are thought to have come into being sequentially; some (though certainly not all) reflect the process of aging on the subject. The reason for the creation of new non-age-related types is not known and is the subject of much discussion. It has been generally thought that new portrait types of an emperor or empress were created for special occasions, such as a great victory or the award of a new title; Fittschen famously suggested that each of Faustina's different portrait types was created to mark the birth of a new child.[48] There is, however, no ancient evidence on the subject of portrait type creation, and alternate processes to the

44. Champlin 1974, 136.
45. Fündling 2016.
46. Levick 2014, 13–14.
47. Trans. M. Staniforth, Harmondsworth, England, 1964.
48. Fittschen 1982. See Chapters 6 and 7 for detailed discussion.

standard theory of "great event = new portrait type" can be imagined.[49] For whatever reason they were initially created, it is clear that through a process of careful copying these portrait types were distributed throughout the empire. The general idea is that models would be sent out from Rome, and these would then be replicated in the provinces. This process gives the name to individual members of a specific type: replicas. Sometimes, through an imperfect copying process, or through the influence of local taste or style, variations might be made to these "official" types; these are called variants. A variant need not arise in a far-flung province; there is clear evidence from Faustina's numismatic portraiture that such a change in portrait type could occur in Rome itself.

Die analysis offers two important opportunities to increase our understanding of Faustina's portraiture. The first comes from the ability to reconstruct a clear chronological sequence not only of the types, but also of their individual replicas (the individual dies on which they were engraved) and thus to document in great detail any processes of change that occur. The second is the ability to contextualize these observed changes in portrait type in the iconographic framework of the reverse typology. That is to say, it is possible to see if changes in portrait type occurred at the same time as changes in the images on the reverse of the coinage (or not), and thus (perhaps) to suggest possible reasons for the changes—and, of course, to evaluate earlier theories.

49. An excellent critique of the history of thought on portrait type creation is given by Fejfer 1998.

Chapter 2

VENVS GENETRIX: Faustina's First Child

Portrait Type 1

Faustina the Younger began her life on the public stage from a position of significant strength. She was descended from a *diva*, Matidia, Trajan's niece (and later, after the death of her mother Faustina the Elder, gained another *diva* in her lineage).[1] And of course her mother, Faustina the Elder, had been deified only recently and was currently being given public prominence in Rome.[2] Although Faustina the Younger was not granted divine status in her own right in Rome, in the Greek east she was already known as Nea Faustina, meaning "the new goddess Faustina" (in this nomenclature, "Faustina" refers to Diva Faustina, the Elder).[3] Faustina the Younger was married to Marcus Aurelius in 145; we have a record of this event in the municipal calendar of Ostia, the *Fasti Ostienses* (tablet Pa, ll. 3–5; this calendar, a list of important events in Ostia and Rome, was inscribed on marble slabs and publicly exhibited at Ostia; not all slabs are preserved and many are broken, thus the record is fragmentary):

> [---]as Annia Faustina M. Aurelio Caesari nupsit. [---
>
> [imp. A]ntoninus Aug. congiar(ium) dedit (denarios) C. III id. Mai dies promi[ssos]
>
> [---ed]ere coepit.

"[on an unknown day in an unknown month] Annia Faustina married Marcus Aurelius Caesar. Imperator Antoninus Augustus gave a *congiarium* of 100 *denarii*. Three days before the Ides of May, he began to give the [unknown number of] days of games which had been

1. Levick 2014, 58.
2. On Diva Faustina, see Beckmann 2012.
3. On Nea as a title, see Hahn 1994, 313. The tradition stretched back into the Hellenistic period and encompassed many female members of the imperial family. Livia, for example, as known as Nea Aphrodite.

promised."[4] The marriage was commemorated on *aurei* struck in the name of Marcus Caesar, where he is named consul for the second time (COS II), which office he entered in January 145.[5] The reverse is inscribed VOTA PVBLICA and depicts a man and a woman—Marcus and Faustina—joining hands in the presence of Concordia. This is the first appearance of Faustina the Younger on a coin; we must wait two years to see her there again. This record in the *Fasti Ostienses* is also important from another point of view: as evidence of a connection between coins and special events. The *congiarium* was a distribution of money by the emperor to the *plebs* at Rome. This ceremony would have put coins directly into the hands of the people, and we might imagine them paying particular attention to the types they bore.[6]

The next major event in Faustina's life was the birth of her first child, a daughter. We know from the *Fasti Ostienses* (Pb.13–15) that this happened on the last day of November in AD 147, and that the very next day, on 1 December, Faustina was named "Augusta":

> [-]X k. April. aqua magna fuit. Pr. k. Dec. Aurelio Caesar(i) / [ex A]nnia Faustina filia nata est. K. Decem. Aurelius Caesar / [trib(uniciam)] pot(estatem) iniit et Faustina Aug(usta) cognominata est.

"10 [or fewer] days before the Kalends of April there was a great flood. One day before the Kalends of December a daughter was born by Annia Faustina to Aurelius Caesar. On the Kalends of December Aurelius Caesar entered the tribunician power and Faustina was named Augusta." So the *Fasti* record that on the very next day after Faustina gave birth to a daughter, both the father and the mother were honored with special offices. Marcus assumed his first tribunician power, while Faustina was named "Augusta." This resulted in the curious situation that while Faustina was now Augusta, Marcus remained only Caesar; he would not become Augustus until the death of his adoptive father Antoninus Pius. This may be, as suggested by Rachel Meyers, because the blood ties to Pius gave Faustina a closer link than Marcus to the imperial power.[7]

The birth of her first child and her subsequent promotion to the rank of Augusta appear to have provided the occasion for the first coins struck in Faustina's name. The beginning of Faustina's gold coinage is documented by a relatively long chain (Chain 1) of 45 linked *aureus* dies (20 obverse, 25 reverse), all employing the obverse legend in the dative case FAVSTINAE AVG PII AVG FIL: "to/for Faustina Augusta, daughter of Pius Augustus" (designated by Mattingly as "fa," this abbreviation is also used here to identify all dies bearing this legend). The beginning of die Chain 1 is illustrated in Fig. 2.1. Each die is illustrated with an image of an actual coin struck by that die; the die designations are given in letters and numbers in the lower left and right corner of each die illustration (lower-case letters for obverse dies, upper-case for reverse dies). The die numbers run sequentially in the order that the dies were identified in the die study: they do not have any chronological significance. Thus the

---

4. Vidman 1982, 125.
5. *RIC* III Pius 434.
6. For recipients of a *congiarium* interacting with the coins they receive, see Beckmann 2018.
7. Meyers 2016, 502.

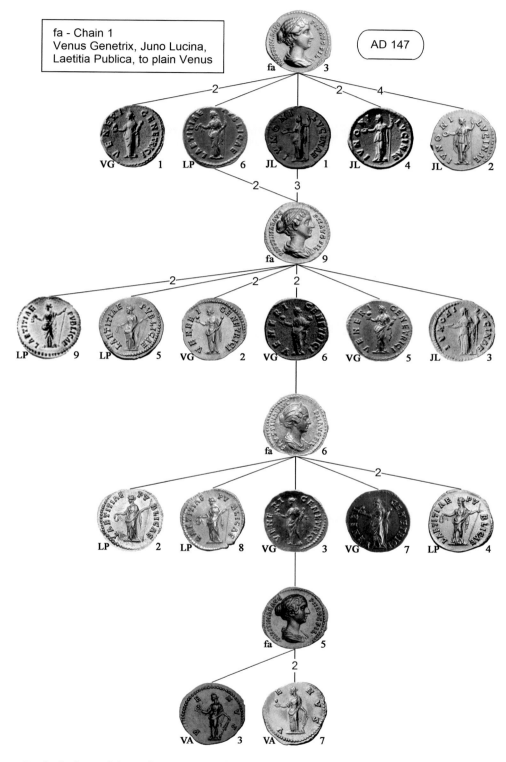

Figure 2.1. Die link chart of the earliest portion of Faustina's coinage.

Figure 2.2. *Aureus* of Faustina showing Venus Genetrix (**VG7/fa6**, ANS 1965.66.32). 18.5 mm. Scale 2:1.

Figure 2.3. *Aureus* of Faustina showing Juno Lucina (**JL1/fa9**, ANS 1958.223.1). 19.5 mm. Scale 2:1.

Figure 2.4. *Aureus* of Faustina showing Laetitia Publica (**LP6/fa3**, ANS 1958.223.2). 18.0 mm. Scale 2:1.

obverse die indicated by the die link chart to be the earliest (at the top) is fa3, while the next obverse die in the chronological sequence is fa9. The lines between the die illustrations indicate links; numbers on those lines indicate the number of coins known for that particular die combination (if there is no number, then the die combination is represented by one coin).

The extremely high quality of the two obverse dies at the beginning of the sequence suggests that we are dealing with the first portrait dies ever cut for Faustina's *aurei* (fa9 is illustrated in detail in Fig. 2.3, fa3 in Fig. 2.4). This is Faustina's first attested official portrait type, though it is possible, and indeed likely, that other portraits were commissioned earlier, for example on the occasion of her wedding. Marcus Trunk believes that he can identify such an early portrait in a small group of marble busts, but without the evidence of inscriptions (or coins) it is impossible to prove.[8] At any rate, Faustina's first numismatic portrait type is

8. Trunk 1999.

Figure 2.5. *Denarius* of Caesar showing Venus Genetrix (ANS 1937.158.293). Scale 2:1.

Figure 2.6. *Aureus* of Hadrian showing Venus Genetrix (*BMCRE* III Hadrian 529; copyright Trustees of the British Museum). Scale 2:1.

Figure 2.7. *Denarius* of Sabina showing Venus Genetrix (ANS 1944.100.45590). 17 mm. Scale 2:1.

distinguished by a complicated hair arrangement. Its key features are four looping bangs; these are gathered up in a long braid that in turn is wrapped into a bun at the back of her head.

The linked dies show that Faustina's earliest *aureus* coinage began with three reverse types all unambiguously connected to the theme of childbirth. With this in mind, it appears almost certain that her gold coins were initially struck in December of 147 or very shortly thereafter. These three types are: VENERI GENETRICI (denoted here by the abbreviation VG, showing Venus holding an apple in her right hand, a swaddled child cradled in her left arm; Fig. 2.2); IVNONI LVCINAE (JL, Juno holding a patera and a tall staff; Fig. 2.3); and LAETITIAE PVBLICAE (LP, a female holding a garland and a tall staff; Fig. 2.4). Almost all known Venus, Juno, and Laetitia dies can be linked into this sequence, suggesting a period of intense coin production.

The most remarkable of all these types is that of Venus Genetrix, "Venus the Bearer." Although Venus was, through Aeneas, one of the two divine progenitors of the Roman people, this particular "version" of the goddess was a creation of Julius Caesar, who viewed Venus as his own personal family ancestor and who built her a temple as the centerpiece of his new Forum Iulium, the first of the Imperial Fora. Caesar made the vow to build the temple on the eve of the battle of Pharsalus, as Appian recounts: "He offered sacrifice at midnight and invoked Mars and his own ancestress, Venus (for it was believed that from Aeneas and his son, Iulus, was descended the Julian race, with a slight change of name), and he vowed that he would build a temple in Rome as a thank-offering to her as the Bringer of Victory if everything went well."[9] Once built the temple became known as that of Venus Genetrix, rather than Venus Victrix; its cult statue was said by Pliny to have been made by the sculptor Arcesilaus, who was so admired that his clay models sold for more "than the finished works of others."[10]

Caesar may have integrated the attributes of "Venus the Conqueror" into the image of the goddess enshrined in his new temple. On many coins of the year 44 BC, a figure of Venus is shown in slightly different poses with slightly differing attributes; sometimes she leans on a shield that that rests on a globe while holding a staff on her left shoulder; other times she leans on a staff with a star or a shield below; in all cases, however, on her extended right hand she holds a small figure of Victory (Fig. 2.5). On the coinage of Caesar this figure is not named, but she is certainly Venus. This figure does not appear again on Roman coinage until the reign of Hadrian, where she is conveniently labeled VENERI GENETRICI (Fig. 2.6). This is the earliest image of the goddess with an inscription that makes her identification certain. There are some minor differences between it and the depiction of Venus on Caesar's coinage: on Hadrian's *aureus* Venus's staff is vertical, cradled in the crook of the arm, and there is a gorgon's head clearly visible on her shield. But there can be little doubt that these are both figures made after one and the same model, the most likely being the famous statue by Arcesilaus in the temple of Venus Genetrix in Caesar's Forum.

Faustina's Venus Genetrix does not fit this iconographic scheme (though an armed Venus just like this does appear on Faustina's coinage almost two decades later; see Chapter 4), nor does it correspond to the only other image of Venus Genetrix that had appeared on coinage before this date. This was on the reverse of *denarii* of Sabina, Hadrian's wife (the exact date is not known, but it falls somewhere in the 130s). Venus Genetrix appears clad in a clingy garment, which she pulls from her right shoulder with her right hand, while holding an apple in her left (Fig. 2.7). The legend, in the dative case (as a dedication) reads VENERI GENETRICI. Mattingly noted that in his time this image was interpreted as the statue of Venus in Caesar's temple: "The type of 'Venus Genetrix' found only in the issue of 'Sabina Augusta' shows the gracious pose generally taken as representing the famous statue of Arcesilas. Venus, the mother of the Julian clan, is taken over from it as ancestress by succeeding imperial families."[11] But

9. App., *B. Civ.* 2.68, trans. H. White, Cambridge, MA, 1913. Cass. Dio (43.22.2) relates the dedication of the temple. Suetonius (*Iul.* 6.1) quotes a supposed speech of Caesar while quaestor in which he proclaimed the ancestry of the Julian side of his family from Venus. For Venus Genetrix in general, see *RE* s.v. "Venus, 15, V. Genetrix" (Carl Koch).
10. Pliny, *HN* 35.45.155–156, trans. H. Rackham, Cambridge, MA, 1952.
11. *BMCRE* IV, cl.

the same type is used later on (lifetime) coins of Faustina the Elder with the legend VENERI AVGVSTAE.[12] The other version of Venus Genetrix, holding Victoria and leaning on Mars's shield, would appear more suited to a cult statue in a temple built to Venus in return for a great victory.

Faustina's Venus Genetrix is neither of these. She holds an apple, an attribute that identifies her beyond doubt as Venus by recalling the judgement of Paris, the event that precipitated the Trojan War, which in turn eventually led to the emigration of Aeneas to found the forerunner to the Roman state. Venus also holds a swaddled child, clearly in reference to her role as "the bearer." The hairstyle of the figure makes it clear that she is not intended to represent Faustina cradling her newborn while masquerading as Venus; instead, the figure is an artist's conception of how Venus Genetrix ought to appear in this specific context. But is the child merely an attribute that identifies Venus as Genetrix, or is it a specific reference to, perhaps even a representation of, Faustina's newly born daughter, possibly to suggest the goddess's support and protection of it? Given the historical context of the creation of this coin type and its unique depiction of Venus Genetrix, it is difficult to avoid concluding that the baby is indeed meant to allude to Faustina's new child. This is the first instance of what will become an increasingly difficult question in the iconography of Faustina's coinage: whether a child shown in a composition might be intended to represent, or at least bring to a viewer's mind, an actual person. Whatever the case, Venus is now directly involved in the propagation of the Antonine dynasty. In the numismatic context she is aided by Juno Lucina, a goddess specifically associated with childbirth and midwives, and she is attended by Laetitia Publica, public rejoicing. We see a manifestation of this rejoicing at the highest level in the record of Faustina being named Augusta by the senate in the *Fasti Ostienses* and the coins themselves would have served to publicize both the event and the associated divinities to the public.

CONTEMPORARY COINAGE OF PIUS AND MARCUS

The coinage of both Antoninus Pius and Marcus Caesar is, in this period, dated by tribunician power (labeled on the coins TR P, for *tribunicia potestate*), making it possible to date all types to within a single year (the tribunician year began on December 10). It is remarkable that for the eleventh tribunician year of Antoninus Pius, coinciding with the first year of Faustina's coinage, no clear reference is made to Faustina's child. Instead, Pius's coinage dated TR P XI is dominated by Annona (the grain supply) and Salus (health); the only event specifically referred to is the celebration of the tenth anniversary of his rule. On the coinage of Marcus Caesar of the same year (his TR P II) the most common types are Minerva, Fides (faithfulness), and Honos (honor). Fides and Honos should be understood as characteristics of Marcus; Minerva is probably an allusion to his position as child of the Emperor, as Minerva is the offspring of Jupiter.[13] The celebration of the new member of the imperial family was left entirely to Faustina (on the coinage at least).

12. *BMCRE* IV Pius 46.

13. Mattingly *BMCRE* III, lxv. Fronto (*Ep. Graec.* 1.4) compares the relationship between Minerva and Jupiter to that between Marcus and Pius.

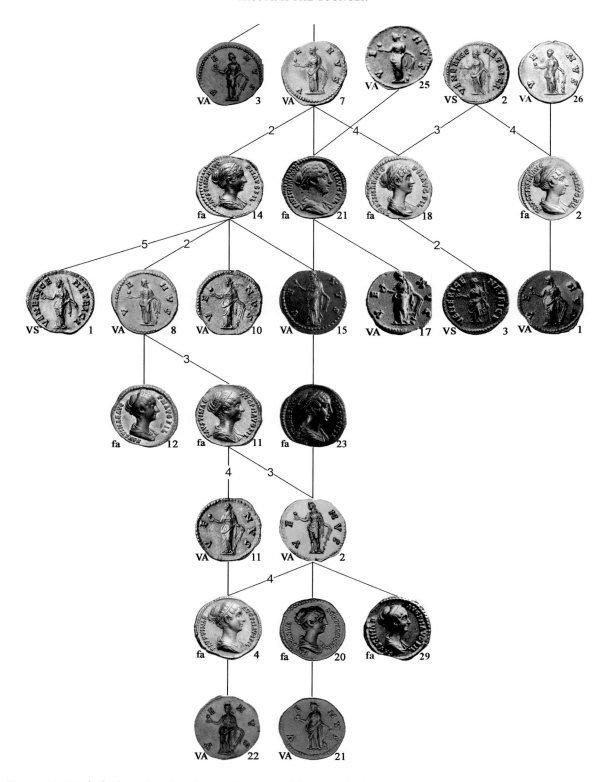

Figure 2.8. Die link chart showing the continuation of the die link chain in Fig. 2.1.

New Types and Changes in Portrait Type 1

The very specific birth-associated types of Venus Genetrix, Laetitia Publica, and Juno Lucina appear to have been relatively short-lived. After only four obverse dies had been exhausted in the main sequence, a new reverse type appears, VENVS (VA, Venus standing holding apple and rudder) (see bottom of Fig. 2.1, continued on Fig. 2.8), that very soon replaces all other types to dominate the entire gold coinage. The legend VENERI GENETRICI continued in use a bit longer than the other two early legends, but paired with a new type showing Venus holding a staff (VS) instead of a swaddled child; only three dies are known, and they all of which link in at the beginning of the Venus-apple-rudder sequence (see Fig. 2.8). At the same time as these new and less-specific reverse types appear in the die link chain, a tendency to abstract and/or misunderstand and misrepresent certain details of the portrait begins, leading to the creation of variants of portrait Type 1. These changes, observable in detail in the die link sequence, are a clear example of how a portrait type could evolve and change through replication. Here, two variants of portrait Type 1 (designated Variants 1a and 1b) are defined; the first is characterized by a distinctly new method of rendering the bangs (fringe), while the second is the culminating phase of a longer process of variation in a number of details (see Fig. 6.27 for a handy illustration of Types 1 and 2 and their Variants). Figure 2.8 continues the die link sequence that began in Fig. 2.1; the chronological order is, as before, from top to bottom.

The first variant to portrait Type 1, here designated Variant 1a, appears in die fa5 (Fig. 2.1, bottom), only the fourth obverse die in the main sequence. Characterized by bangs marked with a distinct "S" pattern, Variant 1a does not reflect a genuine change in Faustina's portrait typology (that is, it is not a genuinely new type) but rather is an abstracted form of the Type 1 portrait. The overall outline of the hairstyle remains the same, but it appears that engravers in the mint had begun to stylize the bangs, employing a shortcut (engraving an S-curve) instead of following the actual arrangement of the hair as seen in the three-dimensional portraits (see Chapter 5). It may not be a coincidence that the new reverse of Venus with rudder and apple appears at this point, and that the previously diverse reverse typology begins to shrink to this one type. Care and attention to detail among the die cutters for Faustina's coinage may have been waning, leading to divergence from her true official portrait type.

Immediately thereafter, Variant 1b begins to develop. It is characterized by scale-patterned bangs, the separation of the bun from the braid, the movement of the bun from the lower back of the head to the crown, and the rendering of the hair between the bun and the braid as a series of parallel strands (rather than plaits as in Type 1 and Variant 1a). The process of change was gradual rather than abrupt and can be seen starting in die fa14 (Variant 1a), followed by the introduction of scale-patterned bangs in dies fa12 and fa11 (Variant 1b), and culminating in the elaborate and detailed rendering of the new variant in fa4, with hatched pattern on the hair in the bun. Variant 1b becomes for a while the dominant portrait form on the gold and silver, but it is rare on the bronze. The new variant is striking in its appearance and is sometimes rendered in high, careful detail, but at the same time it is clear that it is an abstracted version of portrait Type 1 and is not related to any three-dimensional sculptural

model. It is a portrait variant that evolved entirely in the mint. The key evidence that this is a
variant and not a genuine independent type is the fact that the process by which it developed
can be observed in detail in the die links.

At this point in the chain the reverse typology becomes simpler, and by the end of the
chain the only type in use on the gold is Venus-apple-rudder (VA). At the same time portrait
Type 1 appears to go out of use, with one odd exception: a single die of this type (fa25) appears
much later in the die-link sequence, in Group 7 (see Fig. 3.6), at a time when the coinage was
dominated by Type 2 and 3 portraits. It is not an old die re-used, since it does not link to any
reverse dies in the early period, but rather is a newly made die employing an older portrait
type. The revival of "old" portrait types is characteristic of certain later phases of Faustina's
coinage, and this is an early manifestation of the phenomenon.

PRODUCTION AND CHRONOLOGY

The die links indicate that the gold coinage of Faustina II began with a single anvil/workshop
but then quickly expanded to a two-anvil system, a move that could have doubled production
volume. Initially it appears that there was only one obverse die, fa3; at the same time a greater
number of reverse dies, between two and five, were cut (three is a logical assumption, one for
each type). The intention was at least in part to create variety in the typology of the coinage
struck. The expansion of production into a second workshop is indicated by the existence of a
second smaller die link chain (Group 1, see Die Chart 1) that parallels exactly the progression
of reverse types in the main chain (from Laetitia Publica and Venus Genetrix to Venus with
apple and rudder). This shows that the dies for each workshop were kept separate for a short
period. But die sharing between workshops soon began and thus in the later part of Chain 1,
after obverse die fa5, the links become complex, with reverse dies shared by multiple obverse
dies (see Fig. 2.8).

  It appears possible to define with considerable accuracy the length of time covered by this
coinage. Faustina's portrait Type 1 began as early as December 147; it continued through a
period where two major variants of Type 1 developed in the mint. The end of Type 1 portrait
use (and its variants) is probably to be placed in March of 149, when Faustina bore her second
child and dramatic changes in obverse and reverse types occurred (see Chapter 3). Thus the
entire coinage, and all developments in it, occurred over little more than one year.[14] In this
time period, twenty obverse dies were employed to produce the gold coinage, a substantially
higher number than the approximately eight used on average per year to strike *aurei* in the
name of Diva Faustina.[15] This suggests a spurt of intense production, perhaps initially to
provide coins to make up part of a largesse on the occasion of the imperial birth.

14. A double-obverse *as* in the British Museum (*BMCRE* IV Pius 1843) bears a portrait of Faustina Type 1b paired with an
obverse of Pius TRP XII, suggesting that Type 1b was in use in AD 149 on the bronze. Double-obverse hybrids like this were
not part of normal coinage production and must be treated with suspicion, but it is possible that Variant 1b continued in use
longer on the bronze than on the gold.
15. Beckmann 2012, 9. The average is derived from 155 observed obverse dies of Diva Faustina divided by an estimated 20
years of production.

Figure 2.9. *Sestertius* showing Hilaritas (ANS 1944.100.49253). 27 mm. Scale 2:1.

Figure 2.10. *Denarius* showing Pudicitia (ANS 1944.100.49221). 16.5 mm. Scale 2:1.

SILVER AND BRONZE WITH PORTRAIT TYPE I

The bronze coinage employs all reverse types used on the gold, and four more besides, eight types in total. In addition to Laetitia Publica, Venus Genetrix, Juno Lucina, and Venus with rudder and apple, we find PVDICITIA (Modesty) standing or seated, holding up her drapery to her shoulder, HILARITAS (Cheerfulness; Fig. 2.9) holding a long palm (much later to be a type on the gold) and two versions of Venus: one showing the goddess drawing a veil from her shoulder (as on the earlier Venus Genetrix type of Sabina), the other showing her standing with an apple and a staff instead of a rudder; this type appears only later on the gold coinage.

In comparison to the gold and especially to the bronze, the reverse typology of the *denarii* of Faustina is limited. Of the three types (Laetitia Publica, Venus Genetrix, and Juno Lucina) used on the very earliest of Faustina's gold coinage, only one—Laetitia Publica—is also used on the silver. The later *aureus* type of Venus with rudder and apple (VA) is also employed on *denarii*, and Pudicitia (Fig. 2.10) also appears, in addition to the type of Venus with apple and staff. Pudicitia and Venus with staff (instead of rudder) appear only on *denarii* with portrait Variant 1b, indicating that these are later types in this period.

With respect to portraiture, the silver and the bronze mainly follow the gold, with some variation. Most notable is a "sub-variant" of all Type 1 portraits and variants, seen on many *denarii*: in this variant, three bangs are depicted instead of four (e.g., on Fig. 2.10, which bears a Variant 1b portrait, with three bangs instead of the four normal on dies cut for the gold coinage). This is almost certainly a product of the small space available to engrave the portrait, and a need for speed in working, that led to the portrait being simplified by the omission of one bang. Portrait Type 1 is common on the obverses of the *denarii*, as is the later scaly-banged Variant 1b. Portrait Variant 1b, however, is rare on the bronze, the greatest part of it employing Type 1 and Variant 1a.[16] There are two possible explanations for this phenomenon. First, that bronze coinage was produced only at the beginning of this period, before portrait Variant 1b came into being. Second, that the engravers of dies for striking bronze were for the most part not the same as the engravers of the dies for striking gold (and silver, where Variant 1b is common).

CONCLUSION

The coinage struck in the name of Faustina the Younger began with types proclaiming a birth in the imperial family and recording—or encouraging—the attendant public rejoicing. On the gold it is clear that the first issues in her name were exclusively dedicated to this theme. There were no generic types, but only ones that made clear and specific reference to the birth and to its attendant circumstances. It is remarkable that the theme of this new birth was restricted entirely to Faustina; there is no explicit reference to it on the contemporary coinage of Pius or even of her husband Marcus Caesar. Faustina is titled Augusta, but her filiation is also clearly given in the obverse inscription, as it was for Marcus. Her portrait is at first carefully reproduced, with great effort put into faithfully representing her intricate hairstyle, which we know from numerous marble busts. But soon the reverse types denoting a birth disappear, replaced by images of goddesses and virtues. At the same time Faustina's portrait loses touch with the reality we know from sculpted busts, evolving on its own within the walls of the mint into two new variants.

The gold coinage of Faustina bearing Type 1 portraits ends with its reverse typology dominated by one image, Venus holding an apple and a rudder. The goddess is identified by the simple inscription VENVS. The type appears at first unspecific, but as Strack pointed out the addition of the rudder gives this simple image a powerful new meaning. The rudder is "an unmistakeable symbol that the all-controlling Fortuna has now given up her rule to Venus," and that by combining the attribute of Fortuna with the image of Venus, the artist has sent the message that Faustina's Venus now controls the fortune of the empire.[17] Citizens did not have long to wait for a manifestation of this power; Faustina's coinage testifies to another major event, the birth of a second child, less than two years later.

---

16. In the British Museum collection there are only two instances (*BMCRE* IV Pius 1843 and 2161) of the Variant 1b portrait on the bronze coinage.

17. Strack 1937, 112: "ein unmissverständliches Symbol, dass jetzt die allwaltende Fortuna ihre Herrschaft an Venus abtrat." Strack (112, n. 339) also notes that a rudder is an attribute of the particular incarnation of Venus worshipped at Pompeii (though the rudder is held handle-down). On depictions of Venus at Pompeii, see Swindler 1923; the rudder has been associated with sailors, or with an aspect of Fortuna contained in Sulla's patron goddess (Sulla was the founder of the Roman colony at Pompeii).

Chapter 3
CONCORDIA:
The Ideal of the Imperial Marriage
Portrait Types 2–5

This chapter traces the development of Faustina's coinage in the complicated period between the (not quite total) disappearance of portrait Type 1 to the eventual appearance of the very common later portrait Type 5, a simple type that shows Faustina's hair gathered into a bun with no complicated waves or bangs. The die links document this process in detail and reveal a number of unexpected aspects of the behavior of Faustina's portrait typology, including the production of a distinct obverse portrait on a single, unique die. The die links also show that this period begins with a second reference to an imperial birth, signalled by the brief appearance of a reverse depicting Juno with two children. In a striking departure from the handling by the mint of the birth-themed types of Faustina's earliest coinage, this iconography is shared (with variations) on the coinage of both Antoninus Pius and Marcus Caesar. Subsequently the focus of the reverse typology shifts to a theme of marital harmony—or at least it appears to. Close analysis of the types can reveal additional layers of meaning.

A New Birth and Portrait Type 2

The sequence of die links documenting Faustina's earliest gold coinage (Chapter 2) ended with an abstracted portrait (Variant 1b, characterized by scaly bangs and detached braid and bun) and a unified iconographic theme of Venus holding a rudder, perhaps an allusion to Faustina's ability to guide the fortunes of the imperial family. This reverse type—Venus with rudder—provides the connection between the first and second phases of Faustina's *aureus* production, that is, die Chains 1 and 2. Although Chain 2 employs this earlier reverse type, it does not use the same obverse portrait. Instead there is a clear and dramatic change in portrait type, documented by a series of relatively small die link chains.

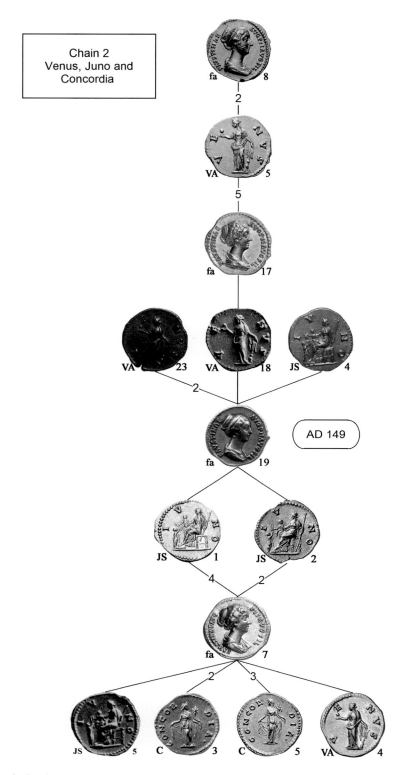

Figure 3.1. Die link Chain 2.

Figure 3.2. *Aureus* showing Juno with two children (**JS1/fa7**; Paris, Rothschild 400).

Figure 3.3. *Aureus* showing Concordia (**C5/fa7**; ANS 1956.184.56). 19 mm. Scale 2:1.

Chain 2, containing only 14 total dies, documents the beginning of this process (Fig. 3.1). Here two important new reverse types appear, probably in chronological sequence (from top to bottom in the chart). The first of these is Juno (Fig. 3.2). The goddess sits on a backless chair and cradles a scepter in her left arm. Her left foot rests on a footstool and her right knee is elevated, although it is not clear what is supporting her right foot. Juno reaches out with her right arm to cradle a small child who sits with his left leg extended and his right leg folded under him; the child wears a tunic and its head is turned back to face Juno. With its right hand the child reaches out towards an object (in fact two objects), held up by a second, larger child who stands on the ground line in front of the footstool. These are two ears of wheat (see die JS2 in Fig. 3.1).[1] The standing child wears a loose, long garment and gathers up part of it with his or her left hand. The legend IVNO identifies the main figure. The children are clearly differentiated in both size and ability: one can stand, while the other merely sits; to any contemporary observing the coin near the time it was produced, the two children of Faustina and Marcus must have come to mind.

At about the same time as the new Juno reverse was introduced another new type appears in the die link chain. This is labeled CONCORDIA (Fig. 3.3) and shows a female figure whose body faces directly out from the field but whose head is turned either to the right or left. She cradles a cornucopia in her left arm, to which part of her drapery is also tied, and raises another part of her clothing with her right hand. Concordia, the embodiment of agreement

1. On one pair **JS3/fa16** (which does not link into the main chain), the child on the ground line does not hold grain, or any other object. It is probable that this coin has been "tooled," altered using engraving tools to smooth the field and increase detail in the relief, and that the grain ears were removed during this process by accident or through carelessness. Tooling is a process used to increase the value of a coin to collectors by "improving" its apparent condition or creating a rarity from a common coin.

Figure 3.4. *Sestertius* of Marcus Caesar showing Pietas with two children (ANS 1944.100.49044). 26 mm. Scale 2:1.

or harmony, was one of the earliest and most important personifications to be worshipped by the Romans. A temple was built to her in the Forum in the fourth century BC, to mark an agreement between the plebs and the senate.[2] The emperor was added to this sphere of harmony by decree of the senate in 2 BC, when it instituted a festival of Concordia to mark the date of the award of the title *pater patriae*, "father of the country," to Augustus.[3] Inscriptions found in the ruins of the temple itself record dedications of gold and silver to Concordia *pro salute*, "for the health," of Tiberius.[4] In the reign of Hadrian, Concordia was a major theme on the coinage struck in the name of Sabina and of Aelius and Antoninus as Caesars; it appears on Hadrian's own coinage in smaller proportion.

Iconographic elements of these two types on Faustina's *aurei*, Juno and Concordia, find striking parallels in the coinage of Antoninus Pius and Marcus Caesar. This is a particularly important observation since the date of these coins can be determined by the iteration of the tribunician power of both the emperor and his designated successor (TRP XII and III respectively). Two reverse types on coins of Marcus Caesar dated TRP III (December 148 to December 149) show two children. On the first, appearing on Marcus's bronze coinage (Fig. 3.4), a female figure (labeled Pietas, below her) stands holding an infant in her left arm and stretches her right arm over a young girl standing beside her. On the second, appearing on gold and silver, two figures, one smaller than the other, stand flanking the personification of Concordia (*BMCRE* IV Pius 680, 681). Fittschen identified the two small figures sheltered by Concordia as images of Marcus and Faustina; Annetta Alexandridis on the other hand argued that they are intended to represent children, and noted that "Concordia" between adults is represented using a different iconographic format (she means presumably the *dextrarum iunctio*, the joining of hands).[5] The top of the head of the shorter figure does not even reach the shoulder of the taller; this is entirely unlike the depiction of Marcus and Faustina on the Concordia type struck on *sestertii* in the name of Pius and Diva Faustina to commemorate

2. Plut., *Cam.* 42.3–4.

3. Egger 1838, 15. *Fasti Praenestini*, 5 Feb.: *Ad Non. Februar. Concordiae in arce feriae ex S. C. quod eo die imperator Caesar, Pontifex maximus, trib. potest. XXI. cos. XIII. a S. P. Q. Romano Pater Patriae appellatus.*

4. *ILS* 153, 3783.

5. Fittschen 1982, 25; Alexandridis 2004, 29.

Figure 3.5. *Sestertius* of Antoninus Pius, AD 149 (ANS 1944.100.48276). 31 mm. Scale 2:1.

their wedding, where both figures are roughly the same size (*RIC* III, Pius 601). The conclusion must be that the figures on Marcus's second reverse type are children, and that one is older than the other.

These images strongly echo two of Faustina's own coin types. Her seated Juno cradles a small child in her lap while a larger child stands to the left; Marcus's Pietas holds a small child in her arm while a larger one stands on the ground. The figure of Faustina's Concordia (Fig. 3.3) is an almost exact replica of the same figure on Marcus's (*BMCRE* IV Pius 680, 681), though without children, but with the addition of a cornucopia. It is possible that this Concordia type of Marcus Caesar was created by deliberately combining iconography drawn from two types of Faustina (Juno and Concordia), which die links show were introduced at exactly the same time. This suggests very strongly that these reverse types should be considered as contemporary, thus dating Faustina's coins with two children to ca. 149.

On sestertii of Antoninus Pius dated to the same year (TRP XII = December 10, AD 148 to December 9, 149) two children's busts are shown in crossed cornucopias (Fig. 3.5).[6] The details of the children's heads present a problem, since, lacking visible buns on either of them, they appear to be boys, not girls. Mattingly noted this discrepancy and attempted to explain it by arguing that twins were born in 149, one Lucilla and the other unknown. Fittschen on the other hand was guided by the appearance of the heads alone and argued that they represent two boys, thus distinguishing this birth from that of Lucilla entirely; this led Dietmar Kienast to include the birth of twins in 149 in his list of the children of Marcus and Faustina (though with the note "Existenz fraglich"—existence questionable).[7]

In this case, the coinage provides powerful evidence for history, but it can only be properly interpreted if we understand the methods by which its types were created in the mint. The coinage of Marcus dated 149 shows two children, one older and one younger; both are paralleled in Faustina's coinage. A further connection between the types of Marcus and Faustina showing these two children is their appearance in the presence of Concordia. The two

6. *BMCRE* IV Pius 678, 679, 1827–1829.
7. *BMCRE* IV, lxvii, n.4; Fittschen 1982, 24; Kienast 1990, 139.

children on the *sestertii* of Antoninus Pius, also on coins dated 149, almost certainly represent the same two offspring. But how are we to explain the fact that, on Pius's coins, the children do not appear to be girls? The answer lies in the derivation of the cornucopias type. As pointed out by both Strack and Mattingly, Pius's type was probably copied from one of Drusus that is identical except for the presence of a caduceus behind the cornucopias.[8] Mattingly argued that Drusus's type commemorated the birth of the twins Tiberius Gemellus and Germanicus in AD 19; naturally the heads of the children were depicted as boys.[9] If Drusus's reverse was used as a model and copied faithfully by the die-engravers of the Antonine mint, then the result would have been two boys' heads on the new type of Pius. Given the existence of three novel types (the Concordia and Pietas of Marcus and the Juno of Faustina) that appear to depict two (most likely female) children of different ages, and one copied reverse (the cornucopias of Pius) with two boys of apparently the same age, it would be sensible to conclude that the new types created specifically for this occasion represent the actual current situation (two female children, one older than the other), while the copied reverse simply indicates the existence of two children. Ameling similarly concludes that the busts in the cornucopias do not indicate the birth of twins, but rather reflect indirectly on the extant children of Pius, perhaps depicted as *genii* or spirits.[10]

Thus it appears that these coins commemorate the birth of a single female child in AD 149, most probably Lucilla. An inscription preserving a list of holidays in the city of Gortyna in Crete gives Lucilla's birthday as March 7.[11] This inscription does not give the year, but Ameling has argued that from the known order of the first three female births to Faustina, this child must be Lucilla.[12] Ameling's reasoning is as follows: with her birthday on March 7, Lucilla could not be the first child born (its birthdate was November 30—*Fasti Ostienses*); Lucilla married Lucius Verus, which meant she was the oldest living daughter of Faustina at the time; Annia Faustina outlived Pius, thus she was alive when Lucilla and Verus married, and was younger than Lucilla (or else she would have married Verus); Domitia Faustina died before Pius (*ILS* 385, her funerary inscription from the Mausoleum of Hadrian, where she is named as daughter of Marcus Caesar), so she must have died before Lucilla married Verus (or else she herself, as oldest daughter, would have married the future emperor). All of this evidence points to the birth of 149 being that of Lucilla, the future wife of Marcus Aurelius's co-emperor Lucius Verus. This means that we can date the appearance of Faustina's Juno and Concordia types in her gold coinage to March 149 or later, and her Type 2 portrait, whose earliest appearance is linked closely to these types, to about the same time.

8. *BMCRE* I Tiberius 95–97, pl. 24.6. For the derivation of Pius's type from that of Drusus, see *BMCRE* IV, lxvii, and Strack 1937, 113–114.

9. *BMCRE* I, cxxxvii.

10. Ameling 1992, 152–156 and n. 43. Strack (1937, 114) reads into these types a more complicated history: first the birth of twins, of which one was Lucilla; then the death of the other twin: finally the types of Faustina and Marcus showing two children, one the older Domitia Faustina and the other Lucilla, the single surviving twin.

11. *IGR* 1509, ll.7–8.

12. Ameling 1992, 151–152 and 156–157.

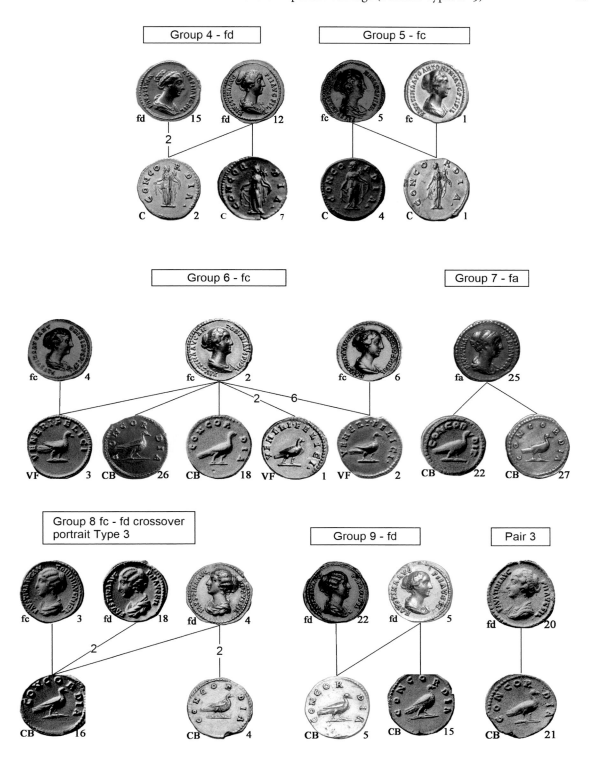

Figure 3.6. Die link groups of Faustina's coinage dating 149–150.

VENUS FELIX, CONCORDIA, AND BIRD

The next major development in the *aurei* of Faustina is a shift to a new obverse legend: FAVSTINA AVG PII AVG FIL (here abbreviated fd, following Mattingly), with the case of her name changed from dative to nominative. We also see the appearance of a major new reverse type, CONCORDIA with a bird (abbreviated CB). This change, however, was not sudden or clear cut, but rather transpired over a period of coin production marked by a confusing mix of different obverse legends, portraits, and reverse types. In particular it seems that legend fd appeared very briefly before a switch was made to legend fc (FAVSTINA AVG <u>ANTONINI</u> PII FIL), which was used for a somewhat longer time before the legend switched back to fd. The numerous die-linked groups are shown in Fig. 3.6. Groups 4 and 5 can be associated with the end of Chain 2 (Fig. 3.1) by their common use of the CONCORDIA/female with cornucopia reverse type. But these two groups employ different obverse legends than Chain 2, which uses the original legend FAVSTINAE AVG PII AVG FIL (fa). In Group 4 the legend simply changes from the dative to the nominative case (FAVSTINAE becomes FAVSTINA; this is legend fd). In Group 5, the legend becomes longer through the addition of ANTONINI (this is legend fc). This legend was also fairly short-lived, with only six obverse dies known; the fact that it was used with the new types discussed below shows that it post-dates the initial, brief appearance of legend fd.

Next comes an important change in the reverse typology, a change that happened in two stages. The first is documented in Group 6, where we see the new reverse type of a bird with a new legend VENERI FELICI, "to Venus Felix." This is only known on three dies. Also linked into this group are two reverse dies with the same type of a bird, but with the legend CONCORDIA. This type (abbreviated CB) then went on to dominate the entire reverse repertoire of Faustina's gold coinage for a substantial period of time. The dove (*columba*) was associated with Venus by the Romans.[13] Vergil writes (*Aen.* 6.190–211) of Aeneas receiving an augury in the form of two doves: *maternas agnovit avis* (6.193), "he recognized his mother's birds."[14] Servius comments on this passage that the dove is sacred to Venus because of its numerous offspring and mating, so the idea of fertility is intimately connected with this association. This connection is also made clear by the legend that accompanies the bird's first appearance on the coinage, since *felix* should be interpreted here, not as "fortunate" or "blessed," but rather as associated with fertility and fruitfulness.[15]

What was the intention when Concordia replaced Venus Felix in the legend? The change may have been made to communicate two messages with one type: Venus and fertility communicated by the bird, marital harmony by the legend. And the dove had associations with a harmonious marriage too. Pliny writes (*HN* 10.52.104) that *columbae* "possess the greatest modesty (*pudicitia*), and adultery is unknown to either sex; they do not violate the faith of wedlock, and they keep house in company. [...] Both partners have equal affection

---

13. C.f. *TLL*, s.v. *columba*, II.B.
14. Vergil *Aen.* 6.190–211, quote from 6.193.
15. C.f. *OLD* s.v. *felix*, 1c.

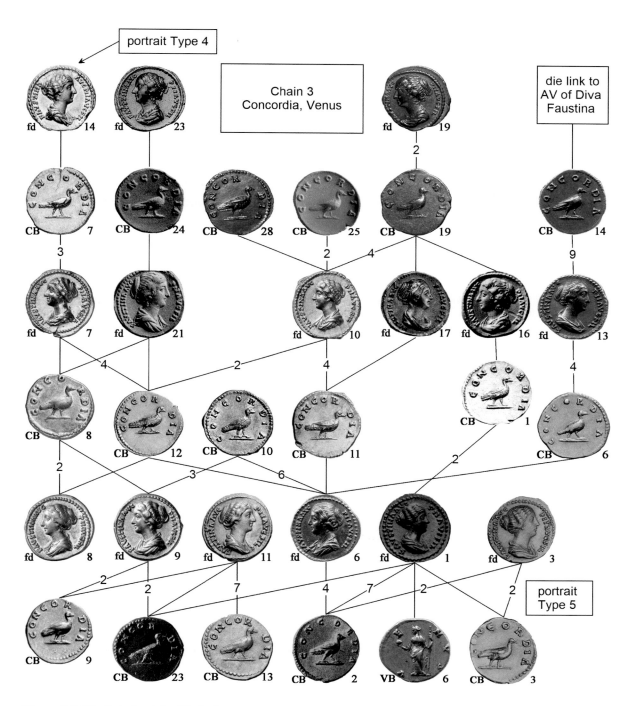

Figure 3.7. Die link chart for Chain 3.

for their offspring."[16] If such a concept was broadly held by the Romans, then what better iconographic motif to choose to represent both fertility and marital harmony?

At this point in the die link chain we also see the first occurrence of a phenomenon that will appear again on Faustina's gold coinage: the "resurrection" of an old portrait type after it had gone out of use. This is seen in Group 7 (Fig. 3.6). The two CONCORDIA/bird reverse dies indicate that this group should be dated later than Group 6, but the obverse die employs a version of Faustina's old Type 1 portrait, Variant 1b. It also uses the original form of the obverse legend, fa. This combination of an old portrait type with an old legend form suggests that this die is the result of copying from an older coin. This is also an example of how we should be cautious when using portrait type as a criterion for dating. While there is a general trend of types succeeding one-another over time, a trend strong enough that it may be relied on in most cases, exceptions are possible and firm conclusions cannot be drawn from isolated examples. It is only when the complete context of any one individual portrait is known that one can speak with complete confidence of its date.

THE APPEARANCE OF PORTRAIT TYPE 3

The change back to obverse legend FAVSTINA AVG PII AVG FIL (fd), which entailed the dropping of ANTONINI, is documented in Group 8 (Fig. 3.6), where obverse die fc3 is linked to obverses fd18 and fd4. At this point Faustina's third true portrait type appears, Type 3. Relatively short-lived (utilizing only four dies), it depicts her with a full-head wave gathered back into a bun. This portrait is not associated with any change in reverse type, but is simply used with the dominant Concordia/bird. The abandonment of the Type 3 portrait is documented in Group 9 (Fig. 3.6), which by its employment of obverse legend fd is later than Group 8. The Type 3 portrait is not replaced by a new portrait, but rather by a return to portrait Type 2. This is a very interesting situation and another example of why caution is required in drawing chronological conclusions from portrait types.

PORTRAIT VARIANT 2B AND TYPES 4 AND 5

After the appearance of short-lived portrait Type 3, the fragmented die-link chain solidifies remarkably (Chain 3, Fig. 3.7). From this point, all obverse dies employ the legend FAVSTINA AVG PII AVG FIL (fd) and all but one of the reverses have the CONCORDIA/bird (CB) type. The die links become complex. Up to now we have seen what has been more or less a linear chain, indicative of sequential production in one workshop (sometimes two) with a relatively small number of dies in use at any one time. The CONCORDIA/bird dies here display a very different pattern: the main linked die group forms more of a dense web than a chain. This is evidence of a large number of reverse dies being in use at one time, what numismatists call a "die-box" model of production. In this model multiple reverse dies would be on hand at any given time and could be used interchangeably, perhaps in two or more workshops at one time.

16. Pliny *NH* 10.52.104. Trans. H Rackham.

Figure 3.8. *Aureus* of Faustina with Type 4 portrait (**CB7/fd14**; ANS 2017.34.1). 18.5 mm. Scale 2:1.

Figure 3.9. *Sestertius* of Faustina showing Hilaritas with two children (Schulman, March 5, 1923, lot 1624).

In the case of Faustina's coinage the number of reverses in use may have been maintained at five, since this is the maximum number of reverse dies to which any given obverse is linked, and this number occurs three times in the chain (with obverses fd10, fd6, and fd1).

Despite the complicated pattern of links, a chronological order is nonetheless clear. Most of Chain 3 is dominated by portrait Variant 2b (with a single brow-wave) and one reverse type (CONCORDIA/bird). But in the lower right-hand corner of the chart, there are two examples of portrait Type 5 (dies fd1 and fd3) and one example of a new reverse type, Venus holding a staff and an apple (die VB6), heralding an important change in the iconography of Faustina's coinage. The dies in the bottom-right corner of the chart for Chain 3 represent the "end" of this dense chain; the beginning thus should be understood to be in the upper-left corner.

Most of these coins use Faustina's second portrait type (Variant 2b), but in the upper left corner is a single obverse die bearing a new portrait Type 4, fd14 (see also Fig. 3.8). In Type 4 (which is also known from medallions and, perhaps, a three-dimensional bust—see Chapter 6) Faustina's hair is arranged in waves as on Type 3, but these are only visible on the crown of her head, the lower portion being covered by a band of hair that is drawn back to a small, tight, low and tapered bun. It is superficially similar to Type 5, where all the hair is pulled back into a small bun. It might be understood as an intermediary type between 3 and 5, except that the die links show that Type 4 (with only the one extant *aureus* die) made its unique appearance in this chain long before Type 5 was introduced, and that between the two lies a dense chain of linked dies dominated entirely by Variant 2b portraits. This is the third example in a relatively short time-span of portrait typology in the Antonine mint behaving in ways that are not explained by the standard theories of portrait type creation and use.

Silver and Bronze

Only variants of Type 2 portraits appear on the silver or bronze coinage; that is to say, the original Type 2 with its high, rigid bun, does not appear there. Most of these portraits, as on the gold, are Variant 2b. On the silver, only one reverse type, Concordia standing, is used with portrait Variant 2a; on the bronze, it is used with Concordia seated and two new reverses, Pietas and Hilaritas. The first of these has the legend PIETAS (Piety) and shows a female figure holding a cornucopia while a child stands to the left. The other (Fig. 3.9) shows Hilaritas as a female figure with the addition of a child to each side; this composition suggests a date contemporary to Concordia with two children on the gold.[17] The scarceness of issues from this period, and especially the absence of the original portrait Type 2, suggests a reduction in the production of silver and bronze in Faustina's name.

Three *denarius* and six *sestertius* or *as* types are known with portrait Variant 2b; there is little new in the reverse typology. On the silver are Pudicitia (with legend fa, showing it is early) and two versions of Concordia, standing and seated, both with legends fc and fd. The bronze continues the two earlier Venus types (standing with apple and rudder and standing with veil drawn before face), employs the same two Concordia types as the silver, continues the Pietas with child type, and also employs the Juno type as on the earlier gold. Type 3 portraits are extremely rare on silver and bronze coinage. There is a single *denarius* with that portrait and a reverse of Concordia seated, and a single *dupondius* (*BMCRE* Pius 2172) combines that obverse with a reverse depicting Venus standing with staff, as type VB on the gold (seen in the lower right of die chain 3, Fig. 3.7). No silver bears a Type 4 portrait, but it is used on bronze medallions (see Chapter 6) with the reverse type of a facing peacock.[18]

It is possible to compare the relative prominence of different reverse types in silver and gold in the general period of coins issued under Antoninus Pius (see Appendix 2). This reveals that the main focus, that is to say the types that were most numerous (judged by die count for the gold, by coin count in the Reka Devnia hoard for the silver), in both gold and silver was the same: Venus and Concordia. The repertoire of the silver coinage includes two types that are relatively common on *denarii*, but missing entirely on the *aurei*: Pudicitia (15%) and Spes (17%). The former appears to be earlier, and the latter (to judge by the legend) later, contemporary with the Diana type on the gold (see Chapter 4).

Conclusions

With the birth of Faustina's second child in 149 the typology of her gold coinage, which had become restricted to a single type showing Venus, was reinvigorated. A new reverse of Juno with two children (perhaps representing both extant offspring) was devised, and also at about the same time, a new portrait. Shortly thereafter a second new reverse appeared, depicting Concordia, which was to become the major theme of Faustina's gold coinage in the following period. Initially represented as a personification, Concordia was replaced after a brief interlude

17. Schulman, 5 March 1923, lot 1642; Mattingly (*BMCRE* IV, 380) identifies the main figure as "Hilaritas (or Pietas?)."
18. Gnecchi 1912, 42, Faustina the Younger 35, three examples (Copenhagen, London and Madrid).

by the reverse with a dove and a legend proclaiming Venus Felix. Then Concordia returned to the coinage, replacing the Venus Felix legend around the type of the dove with her own name, thus combining into one type connotations of both Venus and Concordia. The volume of coin production (in the gold at least) remained robust, perhaps even greater than at the beginning, with very many dies cut and used. Coinage in the name of Faustina had become firmly established as a major component of mint production, and some iconographic themes were also now shared between Faustina, the emperor Pius, and her husband Marcus.

Chapter 4
FAVSTINA AVGVSTA
Portrait Types 5–10

This chapter traces the chronology of (roughly) the second half of Faustina's coinage. The die link sequence of the *aurei* is not as complete as for the earlier period, but again there are a number of long chains and small groups that can be put into chronological order by criteria of types, portraits and style. This long period begins in the later 150s with the appearance of the new and long-lived portrait Type 5, and carries on through five further changes in portrait type until Faustina's death in 175. The order of her portraits in this period is often not strictly sequential, and sometimes more than one portrait obverse is used simultaneously. The most dramatic changes in typology, epigraphy, and portraiture are concentrated in the earlier part of this period, a time of higher production of coins in her name; in the later 160s the volume of coins produced appears to have declined. Highlights of this period include the documentation of a number of births (including the twins Commodus and Antoninus), an increased complexity in the employment of different portrait types by the mint, and the apparent elevation of Faustina's public image to a new level of independence before the death of Antoninus Pius.

Portrait Types 5 and 6: The Die-Link Sequence

Portrait Type 5, a simple style showing Faustina's hair pulled back into a bun, is well documented by die links. These allow us to see that its appearance on the gold coinage is directly connected to the introduction of a new reverse type, Venus holding an apple and a staff (here abbreviated VB, a type that appears earlier on the silver and bronze coinage). The introduction of the new obverse and reverse types can be seen in the bottom right corner of Chain 3 (Fig. 3.7). Very quickly the CONCORDIA/bird reverse type vanishes, being completely replaced by Venus

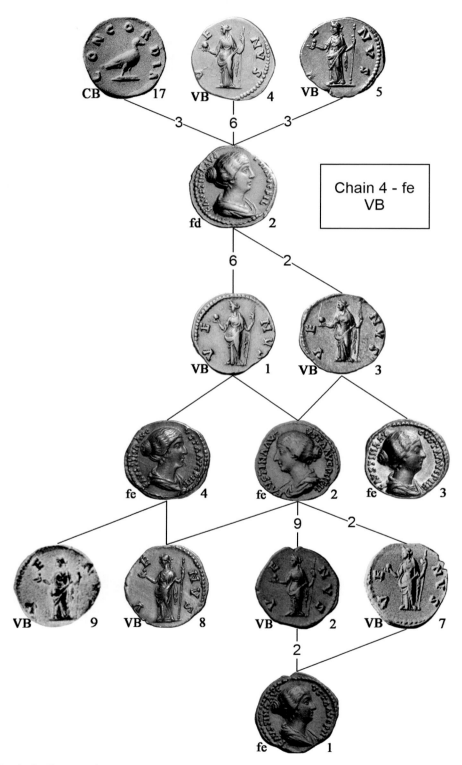

Figure 4.1. Die link Chain 4, showing new type Venus.

(Fig. 4.1); this type continues for some time as the only reverse in use on the gold coinage, until it is replaced by the type of Diana. The nature of the die links also changes, from the complex linkages of Chain 3 to the much simpler and linear linkage in Chain 4. This suggests a modification in the operations of the mint, perhaps connected to a reduction in volume of gold coinage in the name of Faustina. Only nine of these Venus dies are known; one links into the end of Chain 3 (Fig. 3.7) and all others are linked in Chain 4 (Fig. 4.1). The chronological order of Chain 4 is made clear by two factors: the linkage of one CONCORDIA/bird reverse at one end of the chain (indicating the beginning), and a change in obverse legend from fd (dominant in Chain 3) to fe (with AVGVSTA spelled out in full).

Reverse type Venus, apple and staff (VB) is relatively short lived and is soon replaced by Diana (AD), showing the goddess standing holding a bow and arrow; accompanying it is a major change in the arrangement of the legend and, it seems, the introduction of the new Type 6 portrait (see Groups 10 and 11 in Die Chart 5 and Chain 6 in Fig. 4.2). The obverse legend is now simply FAVSTINA AVGVSTA, and the reverse gives the continuation of her nomenclature as AVGVSTI PII FIL(ia). The portrait is characterized by a remarkable waved hair pattern. Tightly curved lines run from the crown of Faustina's head towards her face, becoming ever more closely spaced. The Type 6 portraits also receive a fresh treatment of the drapery. Its wider expanse compared to earlier versions is characterized by diagonal folds on both shoulders that frame a v-shaped neckline on Faustina's upper chest.

The die links suggest that both the new portrait and the new Diana reverse type were introduced at about the same time. The links also make clear that the old portrait Type 5 did *not* go out of use at this time (see Chain 5 in Die Chart 2, continued on the right side of Fig. 4.2). Instead, both portrait types were employed simultaneously together with the Diana reverse (Fig. 4.2), but there are no links between the two different portrait types. The key chronological indicator here is exact synchronization of the disappearance of Faustina's filiation in both chains at the same time as the type of Diana goes out of use. Such a major change in Faustina's nomenclature must have been implemented on all coin types across the entire mint; the pattern seen in the die links can only have come about if these two chains were created simultaneously. The lack of links between the two different portrait types shows that a specific group of reverse dies was paired with obverse dies bearing the two different portraits. That is to say, all obverses with Type 5 portraits link together (Chain 5), and all obverses with Type 6 portraits do likewise (Groups 10 and 11 on Die Chart 5 and Chain 6 in Fig. 4.2). This evidence all points to the existence of two discrete but parallel workshops in the mint, each with its own distinct group of dies which were not shared with the other workshop. This separation of dies could have been achieved by a number of possible methods: by segregating them in different physical spaces, for example, or by establishing a careful control system in a central die storage area. The parallel workshops continued producing coins, well documented in the two parallel die link chains: Chain 5, using portrait Type 5 obverse dies, and Chain 6, using Type 6 portraits. Both chains begin with the then-ubiquitous Diana (AD) reverse. Then, in a dramatic epigraphic change, Faustina's filiation suddenly vanishes from the coinage. At the exact same time two new reverse types are introduced: FECVNDITATI AVGVSTAE (FE, showing a standing female with three children) and DIANA LVCIF(era); abbreviated here

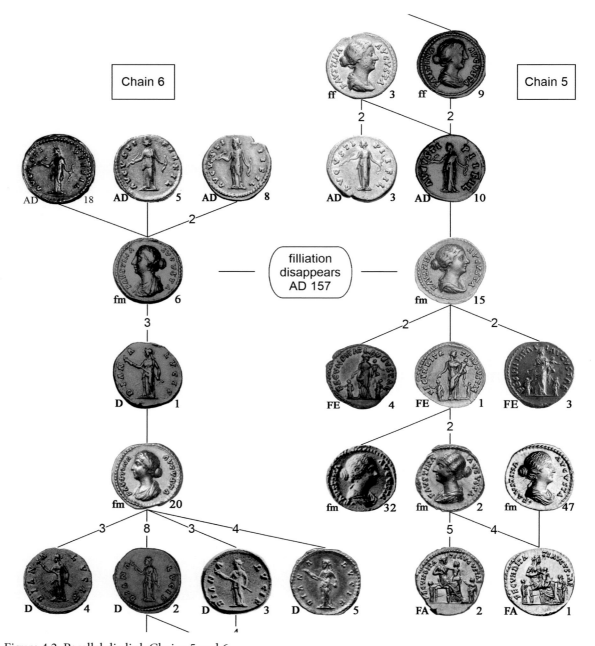

Figure 4.2. Parallel die link Chains 5 and 6.

as D, showing the goddess holding a torch. Die FE1 (on the right side of Fig. 4.2) appears of higher artistic quality and detail than the others and may be a master die. This observation is strengthened by the fact that on FE1 the main figure rests her weight on her left leg, while on the other dies it is on her right leg; this mirroring may be the result of copying from a coin produced by FE1. The die links show that these two reverses continued to be used in separate workshops, Fecunditas being confined to Chain 5 with its Type 5 portraits and Diana Lucifera

Figure 4.3. *Aureus* of Faustina, portrait Type 5, reverse Fecunditas seated with three children (**FA2/fm2**, ANS 1955.191.16). 18 mm. Scale 2:1.

restricted to Chain 6 and its Type 6 portraits. In Chain 5 the type Fecunditas then changes from a standing to a seated figure (FA), though with the same number of children (Fig. 4.3).[1]

Most scholars have assumed that Faustina's filiation would have been dropped from the coin legends when her father, Antoninus Pius, died. But instead the die links show that it coincided exactly with the introduction of the two new reverses, Fecunditas and Diana Lucifera, both presumably referencing a new birth in the imperial household. As a result of this change Faustina was no longer presented as the daughter of Antoninus Pius, but rather simply as "Faustina Augusta;" this marked a significant development in the public image of the empress. A fairly precise date for this event appears to be given by a hoard of *aurei* found in Egypt in the 1920s, whose contents were mentioned by Mattingly and Sydenham in *RIC* III and then published in greater detail by Strack in the third volume of his *Reichsprägung*.[2] The hoard included *aurei* of Pius dated (by tribunician power) to AD 143 (1 coin), 145 (1 coin) 146 (2 coins), 148 (1 coin), 149 (2 coins), 153 (2 coins), 154 (1 coin), 156 (6 coins) and 157 (29 coins). There are no later coins, so 157 is apparently not only to be the terminal date of the hoard, but also the production year of about half its contents. The hoard also had seven coins of Faustina II: 5 of Diana with bow (with filiation given on the reverse), and 2 of the Fecunditas seated with three children (no filiation). The die link chart (Fig. 4.2) shows clearly that these two types were in use exactly at the time when Faustina's filiation disappeared; they mark in fact the exact point of transition between coins with and without mention of her father. The evidence of the die links strongly reinforces that of the hoard, making it possible to state beyond a reasonable doubt that these coins were produced in the same year, and that the year was 157.

Chains 5 and 6 appear to end at about the same time, with the same number of reverse dies (5) being used in each after the disappearance of Faustina's filiation. The next gold coinage to be struck is represented by Groups 12 and 13 (Fig. 4.4) and Pairs 9–12 (Die Chart 5). These employ both Type 5 and 6 portraits, and in Group 12 we see that both portrait types are used, sharing the same reverse dies. This suggests that the separate workshops had now

1. Fittschen (1982, 27–28) dates the FE and FA types to 152 in order to associate them with the birth of Aelius Antoninus. Juno Lucina with three children, however, he (29) dates to 159 based on parallels with Pietas types of Pius and Marcus dated 159 and 160.

2. *RIC* III, 3 n. 3. Strack (1937, 18). Strack thanks Mattingly for sharing this documentation with him, but does not say exactly what form it was in.

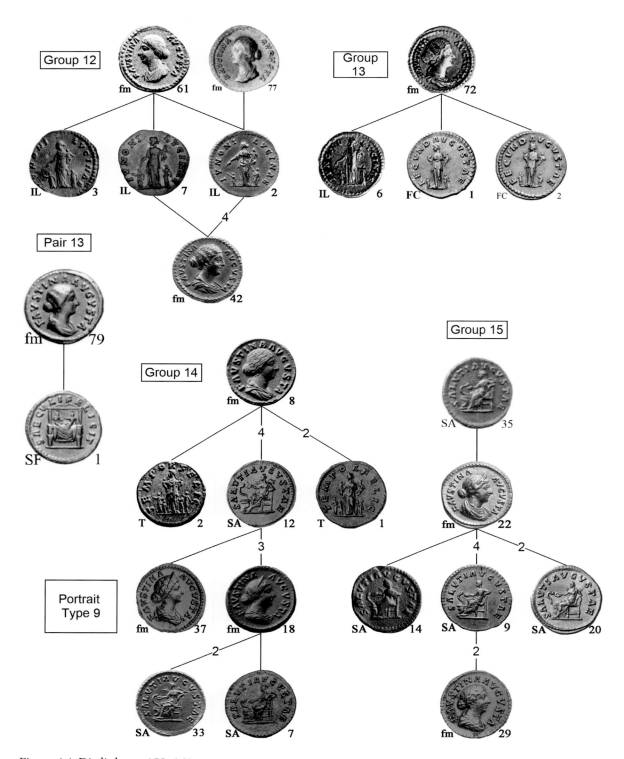

Figure 4.4. Die links ca. 158–161.

Figure 4.5. *Aureus* of Antoninus Pius showing Pietas and four children (ANS 1965.66.10). 18 mm. Scale 2:1.

merged or had begun to share dies. There also has been a change in reverse type, one that dominates these coins: IVNONI LVCINAE (Juno Lucina with three children, abbreviated IL). The arrangement of the figures is similar to the earlier Fecunditas type (FE), but the adult figure's head is turned left, the smaller standing child (when there is a clear difference) is on the left rather than the right, and the cradled child is smaller and more sketchily rendered. Portrait Type 6 (wavy incised lines expanding from crown towards face) is combined with the reverse type showing three children (legend IVNONI LVCINAE), but never afterwards. The latest possible date of its use on Faustina's *aurei* is thus AD 160, and it may have gone out of use somewhat earlier.

From the year 157 Faustina's gold coinage was dominated by the iconographic theme of a female figure with three children. Then, in die linked Group 13, a dramatic change occurs: a new reverse, FECVND(itati) AVGVSTAE, Fecunditas with four children (FC, upper right in Fig. 4.4), is linked to Juno Lucina (die IL6) with three children. The very same iconographic type—a female figure with four children but with the legend PIETATI AVG—appears on coinage of all metals of Antoninus Pius and Marcus Caesar dated from December 10, 160 and later (Fig. 4.5). This is the tribunician year in which Pius died (on March 7, 161), so these coins must pre-date his death.[3] The addition of a fourth child to the previously dominant iconographic schema of three children, along with the legend change on Faustina's coinage to Fecunditas, may have been intended to represent the birth of a single child, a child distinct from the twins Fulvus Antoninus and Commodus who were born to Faustina the next year, on August 31, 161.[4]

SILVER AND BRONZE WITH PORTRAIT TYPE 5

The *denarius* repertoire with Type 5 portraits is large, but it must be noted that this portrait remained in use on *denarii* well into the time when the *aureus* coinage had already largely moved on to Type 7 and 8 portraits. This late survival of the Type 5 portrait is made clear by the existence of many obverse dies that employ the "all-round" style of legend characteristic of the years immediately following the death of Antoninus Pius (see discussion of the coinage of

3. Pietas with four children on coins of Antoninus Pius: *BMCRE* Pius 1012–1015, 2109–2110; of Marcus Caesar: *BMCRE* Pius 1019–1021, 2123.
4. Strack (1937, 122) dates the birth of this single child to summer 160.

Figure 4.6. *Denarius* of Faustina with Fecunditas and four children (ANS 1956.127.950). 17.5 mm. Scale 2:1.

Figure 4.7. *Denarius* of Faustina with two children on throne (ANS 1948.19.1348). 17.5 mm. Scale 2:1.

AD 161–163 below), and by the employment of a number of reverse types that likewise belong to a later part of the gold coinage repertoire.

The earliest Type 5 *denarii* have the reverse type of standing Concordia. This is followed, together with a change to obverse legend FAVSTINA AVGVSTA, by three types with reverse legend AVGVSTI PII FIL: Concordia, Spes, and Venus. The Type 6 portrait that is very common on the gold coinage of the same period never appears on the silver. Next in chronological order (as can be determined by the dropping of Faustina's filiation from the reverse legend) are types showing seated Concordia and Diana Lucifera, the latter reflecting the same type on the gold. Then come three types that are associated with all-round legends on the obverse: Fecunditati Augustae, "to the fruitfulness of the empress," with four children attending the personification (Fig. 4.6); Saeculi Felicitati, "to the happiness (or fruitfulness) of the age," with two children on a throne (Fig. 4.7); and Temporum Felicitati, "to the happiness of the times," with six children accompanying a female personification (paralleling type T on the gold in Fig. 4.4, part of the interesting late Group 14 where two obverse dies bearing Type 5 portraits are linked to one with a Type 9 portrait). Venus standing with apple and staff rounds out the group employing all-round obverse legends on the silver.

Bronze coins with Type 5 portraits, obverse legend FAVSTINA AVG PII AVG FIL, and reverse type Felicitas, appear to have made up Faustina's part of an important large shipment of medium bronze to Britain in AD 155, as shown by coin finds at Bath.[5] The core of this shipment was the Britannia type of Antonius Pius, which is almost never found outside of Britain but accounts for the majority of Antonine *asses* found within the province (71% in the

5. Walker 1988, 294–295.

Bath deposit, 213 out of 299 coins). Dated by tribunician power to the same year is a Mars type of Marcus Caesar (58% at Bath), an AETERNITAS/Pietas type of Diva Faustina (59% at Bath), and the Felicitas type of Faustina the Younger (53% at Bath).

The bronze coinage does not employ the all-round obverse legend, a feature that appears restricted to the gold and silver (presumably the die-engraver responsible for the precious metals did not work on dies for the bronze). Nonetheless, the employment of two relatively late *aureus* reverse types (Saluti Augustae, as SA on the gold in Fig. 4.4, and Temporum Felicitati, as T on the gold) suggests that, as on the silver, portrait Type 5 tended to be longer lived on the bronze than on the gold. Again like the silver, the bronze coinage of Faustina lacks portrait Type 6; Type 5 may have been employed in its stead. The earliest reverse type with a Type 5 obverse portrait is Diana, as on the gold but with no legend besides SC in the field; the obverse uses the legend fe, the same as on the very earliest *aureus* dies with Type 5 portraits. Another *sestertius* type of this period is Hilaritas, showing a standing female with one arm raised. These are followed by three types with legend AVGVSTI PII FIL that exactly mimic the types of the *denarii*: Concordia, Spes, and Venus. After the dropping of Faustina's filiation, the bronze shares five types with the gold: first Diana Lucifera and Iuno Lucina, then Salus, Temporum Felicitas, and Juno. In common with the silver are Saeculi Felicitas (two children on a throne) and Fecunditas Augustae (female with four children). A final novelty of the bronze coinage is the appearance of a variant of Portrait Type 5, known to me from only one coin (a *sestertius* in the British Museum), showing a bun with a bold woven pattern rather than the coiled bun normally seen in Type 5 portraits (see Chapter 6).[6] The reverse type is Diana as on *aureus* type AD, but without legend. Thus this unique variant would appear to date to the late 150s.

THE FINAL PHASE OF FAUSTINA'S COINAGE

The use of Portraits Types 7, 8, 9, and 10 covers the entire final period of Faustina's coinage, from shortly after the death of Antoninus Pius in March of 161 to her own death and deification in 175. The number of dies relative to the timespan is lower than in any of the preceding periods; together with the fragmentary nature of the die link chain, this is evidence of lower-volume and sometimes intermittent coin production. The noncontinuous die chains also make the chronology difficult, especially with regard to Types 7, 8 and 9. In addition, there is an initial period in which we again see the phenomenon of contemporary production of dies bearing different portrait types. The die link sequence in fact documents a roughly simultaneous introduction of two of these three types (Types 7 and 8, very closely related), followed by a period of domination of Type 9 (with a brief reprise of Type 5). The established trend is maintained of changing portrait types at the same time as new reverse types are introduced to the repertoire; these new reverse types are often related to fertility, motherhood, or children.

6. *BMCRE* Pius 2184.

Figure 4.8. *Aureus* of Marcus Aurelius illustrating all-round obverse legend dated TR P XVI = December 161–November 162 (ANS 1972.62.26). 18.5 mm. Scale 2:1.

THE COINAGE OF AD 161–163

The fundamental chronological anchoring point for dating the coins in the earliest part of this final period of Faustina's coinage is the "all-round" legend, which is characterized by larger than normal letters arranged all around the circumference of the coin, with no break above the portrait or reverse type. This is most often seen on the obverse (e.g., Figs. 4.6 and 4.7), but aspects of this style (larger letters and no break) can also be seen on some reverses (e.g., in Group 13, dies FC 1 and FC 2 in Fig. 4.4). As pointed out by Strack, this all-round legend is dateable to a fairly narrow period because it appears on coins of Marcus and Verus dated by tribunician year to between 161 and 163 (e.g., Fig. 4.8).[7] In fact the trend begins in the very last tribunician year of Pius's reign, so late 160 to early 161. By 164, coins of Marcus and Verus have returned to an obverse legend that is split into two parts, divided by the portrait. This stylistic characteristic is a powerful aid in dating Faustina's coinage, allowing us to place all coins bearing it in a similar date range. Three new portrait types, two very similar to each other, appear on coins bearing this form of legend. Types 7 and 8 both show a large, prominent wave of hair , marked with a single wavy engraved line on Faustina's brow, which is gathered into a bun at the back of her head. Type 7 is distinguished by having a braid of hair above this brow wave. These types, as the die links show, are contemporary (see link between Type 7 die fm45 and Type 8 die fm12 near the top of Die Chart 6). Type 9 appears at about the same time, or even somewhat before, but then fades in popularity before making a dramatic re-appearance after Types 7 and 8 go out of use. Type 9 shows Faustina's hair arranged in rows (normally four) parallel to her hairline and gathered into the usual bun; each row of hair is inscribed with a single line in a wave pattern.

The all-round legend can be observed on obverse dies in Groups 14 and 15, on Pair 13 (Fig. 4.4), and at the top (the earliest) end of Chain 7 (Die Chart 6). The chronology of these groups of linked dies is difficult to ascertain and, absent the discovery of further links that might make the sequence clearer, impossible to resolve with confidence. The presence in Chain 7 of the all-round legend (on obverse dies fm1 and fm9, the latter illustrated at the top of Fig. 4.9) gives a clear chronological direction for the sequence of links (from top to bottom

---

7. Strack 1937: 11. See e.g., *BMCRE* IV, pl. 53.15, 54.1–3, 6 (AD 161), pl. 57.1–5 (AD 162), pl. 57.6–12 (AD 163; here the letters begin to become smaller again).

as diagrammed). This in turn reveals a somewhat complicated sequence of portrait types: first Types 7 and 8 are simultaneously in use (see Die Chart 6); they account for most of the obverse dies. At the same time however, some Type 9 portrait dies are also employed (see Die Chart 6 and Fig. 4.9). Portrait Type 9 also appears in Groups 14 (die fm37; Fig. 4.4) and 15 (dies fm22 and fm29; Fig. 4.4). The all-round obverse legend also appears on one die in each group (dies fm8 and fm29), putting both groups—together with the beginning of Chain 7 (Die Chart 6)—in the chronological range of 161–163. Because Group 14 also includes two Type 5 portrait dies (fm8 and fm18), it appears to pre-date the beginning of Chain 7; Group 15 (which includes only Type 9 portraits, but also employs the all-round legend) may be contemporary with the beginning of Chain 7.

Group 14 (Fig. 4.4) includes two new reverse types. One, Salus (SA), is a very common type that dominates most coins with portrait Types 7–9: a female figure seated left on a throne, extending a patera in her right hand towards a rising snake, its lower body entwined around an altar. The legend, SALVTI AVGVSTAE ("for health of the Augusta") identifies that figure as Salus, the personification of physical well-being; given the near-total dominance of this type in the die chain that follows, it is hard to avoid the conclusion that this indicates a major crisis in the health of Faustina.[8] The second type is rare and exists only in two dies, both linked here (T1 and T2). It shows a female figure standing holding an infant on each arm; at her feet are four children, two on each side. The legend reads TEMPOR FELIC, probably an abbreviation for *temporum felicitati*. *Felicitas* is a noun made from the adjective *felix*, usually translated as favourable, blessed or fortunate, but its root meaning is fruitful or productive and it is so used by contemporary Latin authors with reference to fields and trees; so it might be here, with reference to time: "to the fruitfulness of the times." Fronto, tutor of Marcus Aurelius, makes close association between the *felicitas* of both trees and people: *leges pleraeque poenam sanciverunt, ne quis arborem felicem succidisset. quaenam est arboris felicitas? rami scilicet fecundi et frugiferi, bacis pomisque onusti. [...] aequiusne est arboribus honori atque tutelae poma et bacas esse quam hominibus liberos nepotesque?* "Many laws have fixed a penalty for cutting down trees that are *felix*. What is *felicitas* of a tree? Is it not flourishing and fruit-bearing branches laden with berries and fruit? Is it more right that fruits and berries should count as an honour and safeguard for trees than children and grandchildren for men?"[9] Almost certainly with this Group is Pair 13, combining a Type 5 obverse very similar in style to fm8 in Group 14 with a unique reverse type showing two small children seated on a throne (Fig. 4.4; cf. Fig. 4.7). The legend reads SAECVLI FELICIT(ati): "to the happiness (or fruitfulness) of the age," echoing the inscription *temporum felicitati* in Group 14, where two children are held in the arms of a standing female. These coins might celebrate the birth of the twins Commodus and Antoninus, which we know occurred on August 31, 161.[10] After Group

8. A direct connection between the appearance of Salus on the coinage and concern for the health of the emperor is given by the coinage of Trajan dating to AD 116, where Salus appears on coins at about the same time as another type recording public vows for the emperor's health; see Beckmann 2007, 84-85.

9. Fronto, *Ep. Ad Amicos* 2.7.6 (Loeb vol. II p. 180); trans. Haines, adapted. Cf. *OLD*, s.v. *felix*, 1 and *felicitas*, 3b; *TLL*, s.v. *felicitas*, II.A. E.g., Pliny, *Ep.* 3.19.6: *agri sunt fertiles [...] sed haec felicitas terrae imbecillis cultoribus fatigatur*, "the fields are fertile, but this fertility of the land is being exhausted by foolish farmers."

10. As thought, e.g., by Alföldy (1999, 66).

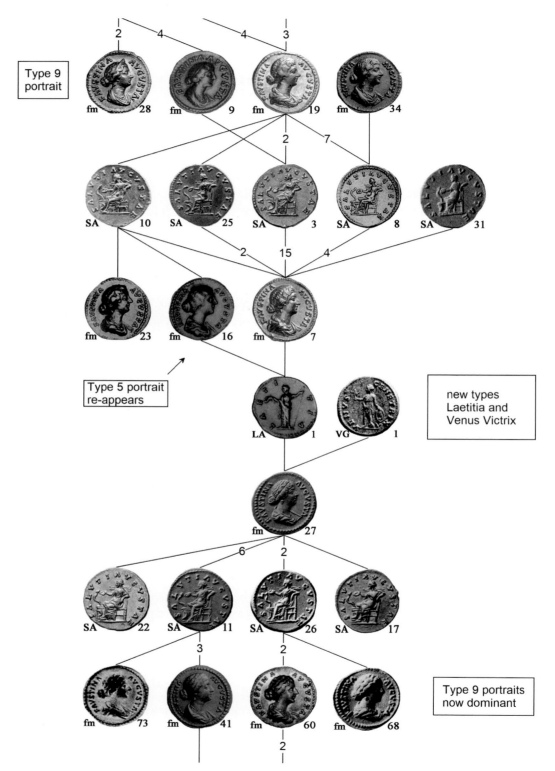

Type 9
portrait

Type 5 portrait
re-appears

new types
Laetitia and
Venus Victrix

Type 9 portraits
now dominant

Figure 4.9. Central portion of die Chain 7.

14 and before Chain 7 should be placed Group 15 (Fig. 4.4), consisting of two obverses and four Salus reverses. The portraits are Type 9, one of which (fm29) has the "all-round" legend characteristic of AD 161–163. When Chain 7 begins (Die Chart 6), it does so with two new portrait types.

PORTRAIT TYPES 7 AND 8

Chain 7 is a relatively long die link chain, containing 18 obverse and 20 reverse dies; the key central portion of this chain is illustrated in Fig. 4.9, which also gives a clear impression of the nature of the portraits and reverse types at the two ends. This chain has a clear linear structure (Die Chart 6, continued on Die Chart 7). The "early" end of the chain is indicated by two obverse dies employing the "all-round" legend executed in large letters, fm1 (seen in Die Chart 6) and fm9 (visible at the top of Fig. 4.9). This end of the chain is also marked by the concurrent appearance of two new portrait types, 7 and 8. These types are very similar, so much so in fact that it is tempting to classify one as a variant of the other, but as Fittschen has shown, they both exist as distinct types in sculpted portraits.[11] Both show Faustina with a single large wave of hair at her brow that is gathered into a bun at the back of her head. The main distinction is that Type 7 has a braid above the brow wave, while Type 8 does not.

The reverse typology is dominated by Salus until about mid-way along the die link chain, when two new types appear (center of Fig. 4.9). One, inscribed LAETITIA, a personification of joy, shows a female figure standing left, holding a staff at the end of her outstretched left arm, and a garland of flowers in her right hand. The other shows VENVS GENETRIX standing left in a tunic, holding a statuette of Victory in her right hand and resting her left hand on a shield. Together these two types (each represented by only one die) echo strongly two of the themes with which Faustina's coinage began back in 147, Venus Genetrix (in another iconographic guise) and Laetitia Publica. The birth of a child is clearly referenced, and the most probable candidate is Marcus Annius Verus. At the same time these two new reverse types were struck, the obverse was changed, though this action is somewhat puzzling. The main obverse portrait reverts from Type 8 "back" to Type 9; at the same time (and linked to the single Laetitia die), portrait Type 5 is brought back for a unique late appearance (die fm16). After these two unique reverse dies, the reverse typology returns to the theme of Salus.

AD 166: HILARITAS, VENVS VICTRIX, AND CONCORDIA

The next chain in the die link sequence, Chain 8 (Fig.4.10), is short but contains three new reverse types: HILARITAS standing with palm and cornucopia, VENVS VICTRIX standing with Victory and a shield decorated with either the wolf and twins (die VX1; Fig. 4.11) or Aeneas (VX2), and CONCORDIA seated with patera. The Type 9 portraits of this chain are very similar in style and detail to the Type 9 portraits at the end of Chain 7, suggesting that Chain 8 follows it chronologically. The beginning of Chain 7 was marked by the presence of

11. Fittschen 1982, types 6 and 8 respectively. For sculpted parallels, see his pls. 42–43 (Type 8, Fittschen's type 8) and pl. 23 (Type 7, Fittschen's type 6).

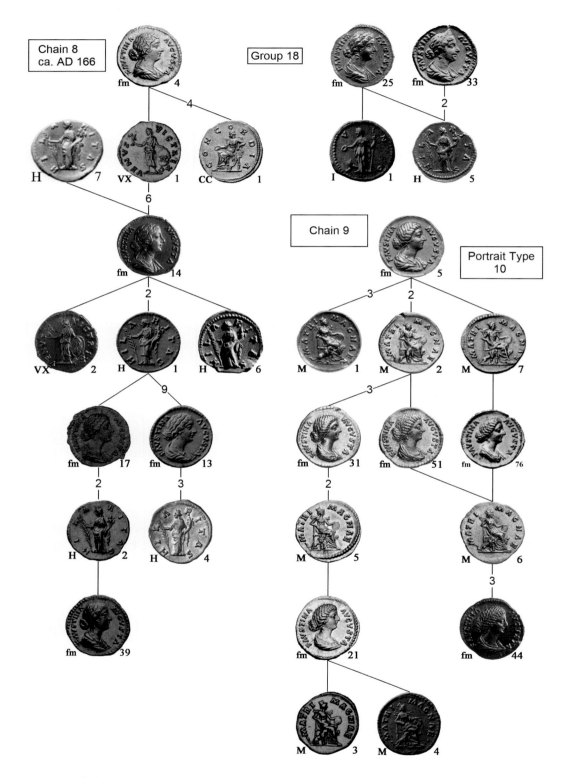

Figure 4.10. Die links ca. 166.

Figure 4.11. *Aureus* of Faustina with Type 9 portrait and Venus Victrix reverse (**VX1/fm14**, ANS 1958.223.11). 19.5 mm. Scale 2:1.

two "all-round" obverse dies (fm1 and fm9), indicating a date ca. 161–163; the end of Chain 7, and the subsequent Chain 8, must therefore be later in date. Exactly how late is suggested by two of the die pairs contained in Chain 8: pair **H7/fm14** and pair **H1/fm13**. These dies are linked together in the center of Chain 8. Two coins struck from these die pairs were found in the great Trier hoard.[12] The latest coins in this hoard are three die-linked *aurei* of Marcus Aurelius dated by tribunician power to 166.[13] This gives a probable *terminus ante quem* of 166 for Chain 8. The three *aureii* of Marcus in the Trier hoard dating to 166 (all struck from the same reverse die) show Victory with a shield inscribed VIC PAR; they celebrate the Parthian victory which he shared with Lucius Verus, for which the co-emperors celebrated a triumph in October 166.[14] Faustina's type Venus Victrix may have been intended to complement her husband's Victory type. There is a difference between Hilaritas, which means almost exclusively "cheerfulness," and Laetitia, which has associations (like Felicitas) with fertility.[15] The addition of the palm branch would seem to specify the reason for the cheerfulness: a victory, as the palm is also the traditional attribute of Victoria.

If victory was the intended resonance of these reverses, it would be a striking example of Faustina sharing in the commemoration of a military victory, an event that until now had remained reserved for the male members of the imperial household. Venus Victrix had first appeared on Faustina's coinage on silver *denarii* in the late 150s (her filiation is still given).[16] This particular aspect of Venus was first invoked by Pompey, who built a small temple to her atop his theatre in Rome, and then by Caesar, who vowed a temple to Venus "bearer of victory" before the battle of Pharsalus.[17] Caesar eventually built a temple to Venus Genetrix in his Forum in Rome, and on his coinage are depictions of Venus with Victory and shield (Fig. 2.5) very similar to that shown on the Venus Victrix coinage of Faustina. This may in fact reflect the iconography of the actual statue of Venus that stood in her temple in the Forum of Caesar. If this is correct, it is evidence of one of the earliest connections between a military

12. Trier 2480 (**H1/fm13**) and 2481(**H7/fm14**). For the full reference for this hoard, see the Abbreviations of Hoards and Collections in Part 1 of the Die Catalogue.

13. Trier 2476, 2477, 2478. All have the same reverse die, the first two also the same obverse die.

14. *SHA Marc.* 12.8 records that Verus insisted Marcus share his Parthian triumph and also that his sons be named Caesar; *SHA Comm.* 11.13 gives the date of October 12, 166 for Commodus being given the name Caeasar.

15. Cf. *OLD*, s.v. *hilarus*, and *laetus*, 1.

16. *BMCRE* Pius 1099–1102, rev. AVGVSTI PII FIL.

17. App., *B Civ.* 2.68.

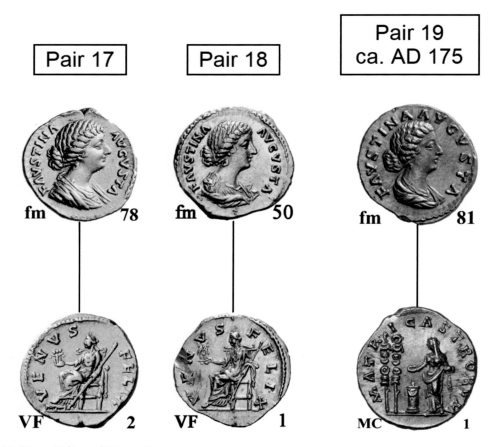

Figure 4.12. Venus Felix and Mater Castrorum.

victory and a female member of the imperial house, a connection that would become stronger under the Severans.[18] The type of Venus Victrix also may foreshadow Faustina's later type of Mater Castrorum, in that it associates Faustina, at least in an indirect way, with the army responsible for winning the empire's victories.

The small Group 18 (two obverse and two reverse dies; Fig. 4.10) links another new reverse (I), Juno standing left with scepter and patera, peacock at her feet, with Hilaritas, showing that these types are more or less contemporary. The proper position of Pairs 14–16 and Groups 16 and 17 (Die Chart 8; all employing Portrait Type 7 and reverse type Salus) is uncertain; they may belong between Chain 7 and Chain 8.

PORTRAIT TYPE 10

Faustina the Younger's final portrait, Type 10, is overwhelmingly associated with one single reverse, Mater Magna, all known dies of which link into a single chain (Chain 9, Fig. 4.10). This portrait is also paired (Fig. 4.12) with two other rare reverse types, Venus Felix (represented

18. Mikocki 1995, 146.

respectively by two dies) and Mater Castrorum. Details of the drapery of portrait Type 10 differ sharply from the latest of the Type 8 issues and do not find parallels on the coinage of Lucilla (thought to have been struck between 164, when she married Lucius Verus, and 169, when Verus died), suggesting that a substantial period of time may divide portrait Type 10 from Type 9.[19] Faustina's last child, Vibia Sabina, was born in about 172, but the type of Mater Magna does not follow the precedent for birth types set earlier in her coinage.[20] Venus Felix echoes the theme, though not the specific iconography, of Faustina's coinage in the early 150s (where the same legend was paired with the image of a dove).

Perhaps the final type issued in Faustina's name on the gold coinage was that of MATER CASTRORVM, showing Faustina as "mother of the camp." This *aureus* type is known from only two examples: one in the collection of the Royal Library of Belgium (illustrated in Fig. 4.12), the other (as yet unpublished) found recently in Poland; obverse and reverse dies are different in each case, and the Polish example has the obverse legend FAVSTINAE AVGVSTAE.[21] On the reverse, a female figure is shown standing, holding a patera over an altar, beside which are two military standards. The type is paired with an obverse of portrait Type 10, and the obverse has some unusual stylistic features. First, the legend is executed in larger-than-normal letters and proceeds around the portrait without a break at the top of Faustina's head (this is similar to the much earlier all-round legend arrangement, though the portrait and reverse type show that the coin must date much later); second, the hair is less finely detailed than the Type 10 portraits in Chain 9, the braids appearing larger and fewer in number. It is probable that these features reflect the time in which the coin was struck, the very end of Faustina's reign, ca. AD 175. Her posthumous coinage exhibits both these features: less detailed hair in her Type 10 portraits, and a legend that sometimes extends all around the top of the portrait (though in smaller letters, due to the addition of the title Mater Castrorum and/or Pia to Faustina's name). Similarly, the coinage of Faustina's son Commodus, which began in 175, also regularly employs a legend with no break above the portrait. This Mater Castorum type is also employed on *sestertii* of Faustina struck during her lifetime, and on coinage of all metals after her death.[22]

The type and title Mater Castrorum is entirely unprecedented; never before in Roman art was a woman depicted in such a relationship with military standards, and never before was such a title given (though of course later, in the Severan period, it would become normal). That this was an official title is shown by its addition to the obverse inscriptions of her posthumous coinage. But while the title itself was unprecedented, the respect that it implies of the common soldier for the women of the imperial family was not. We see this as early as the reign of Tiberius: during the rebellion of the Rhine legions Germanicus sends his (and other's) family members out of the camp for safety, including Agrippina, and this sad procession evokes pity among the soldiers, who recall that Agrippina is the granddaughter of Augustus and "herself a

19. Mattingly suggested (*BMCRE* III, cxliv, n. 2) that the Mater Magna issues may have been posthumous; since Faustina is not called Diva, this is highly unlikely.
20. On the date, see Ameling 1992, 160–161.
21. My thanks to Alexsander Bursche for sharing information about this find with me.
22. *BMCRE* Pius 929–931.

wife of notable fruitfulness and shining chastity."[23] The virtues mentioned are striking: *insigna fecunditas* and *praeclara pudicitia*. They would be perfectly at home in the time of Faustina, a century and a half later. And then later, when after a speech by Germanicus the soldiers beg forgiveness and ask that his family come back to the camp, Gaius (Caligula) is called *legionum alumnus*, "nursling of the legions."[24] This title, casual as it is, shows that an idea of a "familial" relationship existed between soldiers and the family of their commander. We do not know what Faustina did to earn the title Mater Castrorum, but actions similar to those of Agrippina could be imagined: "Meanwhile a rumor had spread that our army was cut off, and that a furious German host was marching on Gaul. And had not Agrippina prevented the bridge over the Rhine from being destroyed, some in their cowardice would have dared that base act. A woman of heroic spirit (*femina ingens animi*), she assumed during those days the duties of a general, and distributed clothes or medicine among the soldiers, as they were destitute or wounded. According to Caius Plinius, the historian of the German wars, she stood at the extremity of the bridge, and bestowed praise and thanks on the returning legions (*laudes et grates reversis legionibus habentem*)."[25] This account gives a vivid impression of the degree to which a Roman woman in the right position might engage with soldiers in the army. Whether Faustina did something similar we do not know, but the long wars against the Germans would have given much opportunity.

Although the author of the *Historia Augusta* implies that the title Mater Castrorum was given to Faustina by Marcus after her death, the coins show that this was not the case.[26] The original occasion for its award is recorded by the surviving text of Cassius Dio, where it is stated that Faustina was given this title when Marcus was hailed as *imperator* following a great battle fought against the Quadi, during which the "Rain Miracle" occurred, so well-known from its depiction on the Column of Marcus Aurelius.[27] In this battle the Romans had been sorely pressed and were saved only by the intervention of a rainstorm. Michael Speidel makes a convincing argument that the award of the title Mater Castrorum was a more or less spontaneous action of the army itself, as was their hailing of the emperor as *imperator*.[28] This new title honored Faustina as protector of the camp, and its suitability was surely developed over the years that the empress spent with her husband on the Danube frontier in the early 170s. Faustina died shortly after she was hailed Mater Castrorum. This type was carried over onto her posthumous coinage. There it was joined by types marking the events of her funeral (an elephant-pulled cart, her pyre, and an image of Faustina herself borne into heaven) as well as appropriate goddesses and personifications (Juno, Diana, and Aeternitas). This coinage did not last as long as that issued in the name of her deceased mother, Faustina the Elder, and was perhaps concluded within a year of Faustina's death.

23. Trans. J. Jackson, Cambridge, MA, 1931.
24. *Ann.* 1.44, trans. J. Jackson.
25. Tac., *Ann.* 1.69, trans. A. J. Church and W. J. Broadribb, New York, 1942.
26. *SHA Marc.* 26.7–8: *divam etiam Faustinam a senatu appellatam gratulatus est. quam secum et in aestivis habuerat, ut matrem castrorum appellaret.* "He [Marcus] was pleased that Faustina had been named diva by the senate, and because he had had her with him in summer quarters, he called her mother of the camp."
27. Cass. Dio 72.10.5. This and the evidence of the coins make it clear that the title could not have been awarded posthumously, as stated in the *SHA*.
28. Speidel 2012, 141–142.

Chapter 5
Portraits: Concepts and Processes

With the sequence of Faustina's numismatic portraits and reverse types established, we can turn to two unresolved questions: what can the numismatic portraits tell us about Faustina's sculpted images, and what did her different portrait types mean? But before we can grapple with these questions, we need to consider critically the concept of portrait types and the practical and technical considerations of their creation, both in the sculpture workshop and in the mint.

THE CONCEPT OF TYPE

"Type" means something different to portraiture scholars than it does to numismatists, even when they both speak about portraits. Numismatists normally define a type as an image having a particular set of iconographic details; thus one type may be Venus standing right with an apple, while the very same iconographic elements but with Venus standing left would constitute a different type. When it comes to obverses, numismatists define types based particularly on differences in dress and adornment, termination of the bust, and direction faced. Scholars of three-dimensional portraiture on the other hand think of type as something else: a group of objects that may be traced back to a single original or model, where membership in the type is determined by whether the individual portraits possess very specific characteristics of hair arrangement and (to a lesser degree) physiognomy. In this definition of a type, the other aspects of the portrait, especially dress, jewelry and (if on a coin) direction faced matter little or not at all. The degree to which numismatics differs from this approach may be seen in the fact that the main taxonomic criterion of portrait scholars, hair arrangement, is normally not taken into consideration by numismatists when establishing type lists.

Part of the reason for the difference in approach to portraits by numismatists and art-historians lies in the fact that the study of portraiture for a long time lagged behind that of coins, with the result that the great value of such distinguishing features as changes in hair arrangement were not immediately apparent to numismatists, who at any rate were able to identify the portraits on coins by means of inscriptions. In his catalogue of the Roman coins in the British Museum, Mattingly distinguished four "varieties" in the busts of Faustina, all based on adornment or the direction that the portrait was facing, while directing the reader to the plates and introduction for more information about "the minor variations of hairdressing."[1] Mattingly was not able to consult Max Wegner's volume on the portraits of the Antonine dynasty, published just the year before, which contained the first thorough attempt to arrange and date Faustina's portraits based on the (at the time) newly-emerging science of portrait analysis.[2] Another factor in the diversion of these two strands of portrait research was the unambiguous identity of most coin portraits, provided as they are in most cases with inscriptions naming the subject. This is emphatically not the case in the great majority of sculpted portraits, and for centuries most of these remained unidentified. Modern typological study of three-dimensional portraits was first developed and exploited to provide these unknown heads with names.

These two separate paths of portrait study have in a number of cases begun to come back together; the most obvious example is Fittschen's study of Faustina the Younger. But this reunion of the study of numismatic and sculpted portraits has not been an entirely happy one, especially when it comes to methodology and interpretation.

THE STUDY OF FAUSTINA'S PORTRAITS

The first and most important point that must be kept in mind when discussing three-dimensional portraits of Faustina is that their very identification as Faustina rests almost entirely on the evidence of coinage. In the absence of other evidence (e.g., portrait statues attached to inscribed bases), the coinage is more or less the only source from which we can learn more about the sequence and meaning of her varied portraits. The history of Faustina the Younger's portrait typology is representative of the development of the study of Roman portraiture in general, and of the way in which women's portraits were treated within this field. The ease with which we today speak of emperors and types—"the Prima Porta type of Augustus"—obscures the fact that even the basic identities of many imperial portraits were not securely known until relatively recently. One of the most famous Roman statues, the equestrian Marcus Aurelius (currently in the Capitoline Museum), was known in the Middle Ages as Constantine, Quintus Quirinus, or even Theodoric.[3] The use of coins to help make secure identifications eventually led to progress, but errors and purely subjective identifications persisted—and still do.[4]

1. *BMCRE* IV, 396.
2. Wegner 1939, 48–50.
3. Magister Gregorius, 4.
4. See Boschung 1993, 1, n. 12. On erroneous portrait identification in modern studies, see Fittschen and Zanker 2014.

In the nineteenth century great advances in portrait identification were made, but recognition of Faustina the Younger remained problematic. In one of the first comprehensive attempts to identify sculptural depictions of Roman emperors and empresses, Antoine Mongez's *Iconographie Romaine* (1826), the Capitoline head of a youthful Faustina II is correctly identified as a representation of that empress on the basis of coinage, but another bust of Faustina is misidentified as Lucilla.[5] John Bernoulli made the next major step in his *Römische Ikonographie* (1891), taking many more busts into consideration, more carefully scrutinizing the coin evidence, and generating sufficiently important results that Wegner later expressed his debt to his work.[6] Bernoulli was aware of the fact that one emperor could be depicted in different ways and used the words "type" (*Typus*) to designate a distinct version of an imperial portrait and "replicas" (*Repliken*) to identify copies of this type. These terms have become standard in Roman portrait studies and are still used today.

Bernoulli pointed to Faustina the Younger as a particular problem, with numerous busts in museums identified as the empress, but on scanty or no firm evidence: "we leave the arbitrarily named busts aside and try first to answer the question, if there is even one certain marble portrait of Faustina, or if we must content ourselves with mere speculations."[7] In analyzing Faustina's Capitoline portrait, Bernoulli noted the correspondence between its hair arrangement and that on coins of Faustina, but then remarked that the profile of the face does not correspond to what we see there, and that in fact it would fit better with the numismatic profiles of Lucilla or Crispina. From this he drew the conclusion that while this particular bust might represent Faustina, he could not agree with Mongez and thus the bust could as well depict one of the other two named women or even a young private person. Bernoulli felt more confident in identifying (correctly as it turns out) a portrait in the Louvre as Faustina, and three other busts as "closely related and possibly representing the same person."[8] With regard to the portrait identified by Mongez as Lucilla, Bernoulli allowed for the possibility that it might represent Faustina but still came down on the side of Lucilla; he gave a list of replicas, though in fact not all of these are of the same type.[9] Then Bernoulli rejected another bust of Faustina (now generally agreed to be her) on the grounds that although its hairstyle does correspond with that seen on coins of Faustina, its profile does not.[10]

Wegner, in his ground-breaking 1939 study of Antonine portraits (*Herrscherbildnisse in antoninischer Zeit*), noted that while by his time there was no difficulty in identifying the male members of the Antonine dynasty, "confusion" still reigned in the question of identifying the imperial women (except Faustina I, whose portraiture is more or less unchanging).[11] The identification of these women could only be clarified, he observed, by closer study of the imperial coinage. Wegner made hairstyle the main criterion for identifying portraits of

5. Mongez 1826, 100–101, 109–110, pls. 42–43.
6. Wegner 1939, 7.
7. Bernoulli 1891, 190 (author's translation).
8. Bernoulli 1891, 192–193. Fittschen 1982, Type 8, cat. no. 10, p. 61.
9. Bernoulli 1891, 193–195. He included for example the head from Markouna in the Louvre, Fittschen 1982, Type 7 rather than Type 8 as in his plate 54.
10. London, Fittschen type 5, nr. 6, p. 52.
11. Wegner 1939, 10. "Verwirrung herrscht nur noch im Hinblick auf die Frauen der anderen drei Herrscher, die Juengere Faustina, Lucilla und Crispina."

Faustina the Younger, placing physiognomic characteristics in a supporting role.[12] He began his analysis with a presentation of her numismatic portraits in order of appearance, corroborated by Strack's recently published study of Antonine coinage. Wegner's faith in the primacy of numismatic evidence led him to identify two types solely on the basis of coins, even though he could find no corresponding sculpted portraits.[13] These were his "Stirnschuppenfrisur" or "forehead scale hairdo" (here, Variant 1b) and an "abgesetzte Stirnwellenfrisur" or "offset forehead wave" (here, Variant 2a). He explained this with the suggestion that the sculpted portraits produced in Rome "were not subordinated to the frequent changes in style," which is to say that Wegner understood the numismatic portraits of Faustina as more closely reflecting the current appearance of the empress than the sculpted portraits. The coins, since they were in constant production in the imperial capital, documented changes in her hairstyle, while sculpted portraits did not (or at least, not as faithfully as the coins). Wegner also offered some suggestions on the reasons for the creation of Faustina's portraits. The first, he suggested, was made on the occasion of her being named Augusta. But the two next types, the "forehead scale" and "offset forehead wave" types, he reckoned were the result of the mint simply attempting to reflect the actual and frequently-changing appearance of the empress.

Wegner identified seven distinct portrait types for Faustina the Younger. This remained the status quo until Fittschen's 1982 publication *Die Bildnistypen der Faustina minor und die Fecunditas Augustae*. Fittschen conducted a more detailed study of Faustina's coinage and distinguished nine portrait types. The main focus of his study was to show that all of these types might be associated with historical events, specifically with the births of Faustina's many children. Thus Fittschen's work presents two theories that require testing: his typology (including its sequence and dating), and his theory for the reason why Faustina's portrait changed so often. Before trying to answer these questions, we must consider the theory behind the concept of portrait types.

THE THEORY OF PORTRAIT TYPES

Thousands of portraits of Roman emperors and empresses are known throughout the Mediterranean and beyond. Most of these are in stone, though originally there would have been many more of metal, especially bronze. Imperial portraits were also ubiquitous on the coinage, and coins are naturally a great aid to identifying sculpted portraits. The study of imperial portraits is based on the identification of types, groups of portraits that can be traced back to a single original model. In theory, both sculptors and mint engravers, in Rome and in the provinces, would have replicated this model, with differing degrees of fidelity, until a new model took its place.

The exact workings of this system are not known, but clues may be derived from the many portraits it produced (we should be cautious here, since an important part of this evidence—bronze portraits—is largely lost). Fittschen proposed that a single portrait model,

---

12. Wegner 1939, 51: "Geleitet durch diese Kennzeichen der Harrtrachten und gestützt auf die ebenfalls durch die Münzprägungen überlieferten Bildniszüge lassen sich die rundplastischen Bildwerke der jüngeren Faustina ermitteln."
13. Wegner 1939, 52.

the prototype, would first be created by a master sculptor.[14] This could have been in stone, clay, or even in the form of drawings of the emperor's head made from multiple perspectives. From this primary model, derivative models for both coinage and three-dimensional portraiture would be created. This original portrait, or its immediate derivations, would then be copied by die-engravers and by sculptors in the imperial capital; then further copies would be produced in the provincial mints and sculpture workshops. Dietrich Boschung proposed wax as another possible material for the original model; this could then have been spread to other workshops, especially in the provinces, by means of plaster casts.[15] Wegner suggested that a "sitting" in the modern sense would not have been required for the creation of a new portrait type, but rather that the public appearances of the emperor would have provided sufficient opportunity for the artist to impress on himself the main characteristics of the emperor's appearance.[16] The same could certainly apply to the empress, and given the fact that Faustina's types are much more clearly distinct than those of Pius or Marcus, the task of the artist would have been easier.

All of these copies of the original portrait model are understood by modern scholars of portraiture to belong to the same portrait type, since all are based on the same prototype, the one original portrait of the emperor or empress. This involved the production of many copies of few originals. Otto Brendel was the first to formulate the theory behind, and the components of, this process in his 1931 study of the portraiture of Augustus, employing the key terms of type and replica coined by Bernoulli.[17] The whole (*Gesamtheit*) of all portraits that can be ascribed to the same model or original (*Vorlage*) is referred to as the type (*Typus*); the individual portraits that belong to the same type are called copies or replicas (*Kopien* or *Repliken*). The term "type" is generally seen as a purely modern designation, but Fittschen has suggested on the basis of an inscription on a herm from Dion that mentions "one type (*typos*)" in two portraits that it may have been current in ancient usage also.[18] Boschung has suggested that the copying of imperial portraits in the same environment that produced copies of *Idealplastik*, sculptures by famous Greek artists, using techniques of reproduction developed in the late Hellenistic period.[19] It does seem clear from the evidence that such copying took place on a large scale.

According to the theory of portrait typology, the reproduction of the type was strict. The theory holds that there was no room for artistic license in the production of replicas of imperial portraits; the only factors that could result in differences between replicas belonging to the same portrait type were variations in the skill of the individual artists or stylistic influences, either because of where the copy was produced (e.g., in a province rather than the capital) or when it was produced (e.g., portraits produced over a long time-span might exhibit stylistic change).[20] This theory has sometimes been criticized for being too rigid, for

14. Fittschen 1971, 220.
15. Boschung 1993, 5.
16. Wegner 1939, 11.
17. Brendel 1931.
18. Fittschen 2010, 226–227.
19. Boschung 1993, 4.
20. Fittschen 1971, 221–222. On the influence of local and chronological style on portrait types, see also Trillmich 1971.

example by Lee Ann Riccardi in her review of Fittschen's *Prinzenbildnisse*.[21] The question of the rigidity (or lack thereof) of portrait typology is a particular problem in the study of sculpted portraits because they are almost never independently identified or dated. This is an area where numismatic portraits have great potential to be helpful.

We have, as far as we know, no examples of the prototype created by a sculptor working directly from the living emperor. Instead we have a great number of replicas of this original; the problem is to sort these out. In his study of the "Actium" portrait type of Augustus, Paul Zanker defined the goal of the student of portraiture as the reconstruction the "*Urbild*" (prototype) through a study of all known replicas.[22] Such reconstruction requires paying attention to the smallest details of the most distinctive elements of the copies, and for most emperors and empresses this means the hair. For this reason, careful study of the appearance and disposition of individual locks of hair forms the core of most definitions of individual portrait types. This makes sense if considered from the practical, technical point of view of the sculptor charged with the creation of a replica. He had the task of reproducing a three-dimensional model using his eye, assisted by a variety of measuring tools.[23] The exact relationship of locks or braids of hair to each other is made clear by their linear nature, and these relationships can be measured and transferred to the replica; the rounded shape of the cheek or the chin on the other hand is not so easy to define and replicate. Thus facial features are much more subject to change through copying and are normally considered secondary in importance in the basic task of identifying types.[24]

This approach to portraiture, especially the focus on typology, has not escaped criticism: Brunilde Ridgway remarked that "Roman portraits are still being studied along traditional lines, and this approach is now somewhat stagnant," then later in the same article called the study of portraiture "basically sterile and fossilized into a single approach," while Elizabeth Bartman more precisely wrote that "[w]hile there is no doubt of the essential validity of the portrait type as a concept, the scholarly emphasis on identifying types has encouraged a narrow, largely descriptive approach that, at least for women, has fixated on hairstyle."[25] The fact still remains that this detailed study is necessary to lay the groundwork and to establish the basic identifications upon which more broadly conceived studies can be based. Here coinage can contribute by providing multiple replicas of firmly identified portraits in their original context and order of production, which all can be used to test some of the basic theories of portrait scholarship. First though, some consideration must be given to the peculiarities of numismatic portraiture.

CREATION OF PORTRAITS IN THE MINT

Two points must be clearly made at the beginning. One is that despite extensive speculation, we have no independent evidence of how the creators of Roman portraits (whether sculpted

21. Riccardi 2007.
22. Zanker 1973, 12.
23. On the exact process of the replication of portrait types, see in detail Pfanner 1989.
24. Zanker 1973, 10.
25. Ridgway 1986, 13 and 22; Bartman 2012, 415.

or numismatic) worked, what models they used, or why they changed from one type to another. Some theories have become so widely assimilated that they have more or less become accepted as fact. A prominent one is the idea that after a new portrait of the emperor was created, this original would serve as a prototype portrait. The prototype might be circulated through the mint and sculptural workshops to serve as a model, or copies might be made and these circulated. This may have been the case, but there is no explicit evidence for it. The only evidence we have is that provided by the copies themselves, the coins and the portraits in the round, and we must work with this evidence and draw conclusions from it. This work must be done without imposing any restrictions based on theories of how these processes may have functioned.

The second crucial point is that whatever methods the mint employed, there is no guarantee that these were fixed and never changed over time. Multiple scenarios can be imagined in which the working process might be altered. New staff might replace old staff, and thus bring new ideas into the mint or sculptural workshop. The officials in charge of coin or sculpture production might also change. And the emperor himself might change his view of his own self-representation as his reign developed. Variation in working methods over time is all but impossible to detect in the sculpted portraits, since the context of their original creation has been lost. But the case with coins, when anchored on a die analysis, is entirely different. Die analysis can reveal not only the exact chronological sequence of the production of the portrait types, but also of the individual replicas that belong to each type (that is, each obverse die).

How were coin portraits created? It must be remembered that the size of the area on which these artists worked when carving dies for *aurei* was very small: about an inch in diameter, and with allowance for the beaded border and the legend, even less space than that for the portrait. The material of the die was steel, presumably annealed, heated and then slowly cooled to soften it before engraving, then hardened later. The tools used were all hand-powered. Roman die engravers worked using a combination of cutting tools and punches. Drills, although they were used to help create some coin dies in the Republican and Byzantine periods, do not appear to have been employed in the Roman mint in the second century AD. Cutting tools were in the form of small chisel-like implements and were used to carve out the bust and to add the details of clothing, hair and facial features. Punches were primarily used for letters, which would be formed by hammering these small shapes into the die face at right angles to create the various parts of letters (whole-letter punches were not used, as can be seen from the varying size and shape of the complete letters). The portraits, on the other hand, were individually hand carved. This makes every obverse die a genuine replica of a particular portrait type.

The material (the die face), its size, and the tools available all contributed to making the process of creating a coin portrait rather different from that of creating a sculpted portrait. It is apparent from the evidence of linked dies that artists engraving a portrait in the mint had two options: to attempt as faithfully as possible to replicate the exact detail of their large, three-dimensional model, or to impressionistically render some parts of the model by using shorthand symbols. Such symbols were frequently employed to represent, in a simplified form, details of Faustina's hair. From her earliest portraits (e.g., die fa3, Fig. 2.4), dots arranged in lines are used to represent braided hair; this shorthand was already in use in the mint for portraits of Diva Faustina. A less-common symbol for braided hair is a sequential x-pattern (e.g., die fa4, in Fig. 6.27, where it is used on the bun, while the lower forehead braid is still rendered with a line of dots).

Conclusion

Given that the numismatic evidence is crucial for scholars of portraiture, it is surprising how long the study of portraits in these two different media (coins and sculpture) remained apart. No doubt the complexity of the numismatic evidence, apparent or real, discouraged portrait scholars from wading too deeply into it. When Fittschen finally did so for Faustina the Younger, he brought with him from the now well-developed field of portrait studies a fully-formed theory to explain the creation of portrait types: that their creation was triggered by special occasions in the life of the person portrayed. The conclusion that resulted, Fittschen's theory of correlation between each of Faustina's many portrait types and the birth of a child, is the most extensively argued thesis to incorporate both sculpted and numismatic evidence. But is it right? Objections to Fittschen's idea have been made but most of these stop short of rejection of the theoretical basis of his work, the traditional theory of sculpted portrait type creation. No further answers can be extracted from the sculpted portraits, deprived as they are of their original inscriptions and contexts of display. The die link chains of Faustina's coinage, on the other hand, offer remarkable opportunities not only to trace the development of her portraiture in detail, but also to contextualize changes in portraits by means of the iconographic repertoire of the reverse types. This offers us an opportunity not only to critique extant theories of portrait type creation, but also to create new ones with a much more solid evidentiary basis, which is the subject of the final two chapters.

Chapter 6
A New Typology of Faustina's Portraits

Faustina the Younger has the second-largest number of preserved sculpted portraits of all Roman empresses; only Livia has more. She exceeds Livia, however, in sheer variety; more portrait types are known for Faustina the Younger than for any other empress. Numismatic portraits are the key to identifying her sculpted images, a fact that appears obvious today but a strategy that took surprisingly long to be fully exploited. Even when it was, by Fittschen in his 1982 study of Faustina's portraiture, the numismatic evidence remained insufficiently anchored in time, causing problems in the correct determination of both relative and absolute chronology. The die analysis presented here substantially resolves this problem, allowing not only a solid relative chronology of Faustina's numismatic images to be established, but also revealing details of portrait type evolution and employment in the mint. The sequence of dies established by this analysis allows us to observe the actual process of coin portrait creation at a very detailed level. We can, as it were, look over the shoulder of the mint worker as a model for a new imperial portrait is brought into the workshop, then copied, and finally reproduced over a period of time. This chapter has two main goals. One is to analyze in detail the system of Faustina's portraiture as it was employed in the Roman mint (a visual summary of her numismatic depictions is presented in Figs. 6.27–6.29 at the end of this chapter). The second goal is to use the results of this analysis to re-evaluate the typology of her portraits in the round. I have tried to restrict the discussion to strictly formalistic and technical issues; questions of meaning are left for the following chapter.

It is important to make the point at the beginning of this discussion that Faustina's numismatic portraits are numerous but also quite distinct. In the past some scholars, even Fittschen, have expressed some uncertainty in the face of the variety of hairstyles on the

Figure 6.1. *Aureus*, portrait Type 1 (die fa9; ANS 1958.223.1).

Figure 6.2. Sculpted portrait, Type 1 (Rome, Capitoline Museum inv. 449, Fittschen 1982, cat. 19; DAI-ROM-38.1445).

coinage as to exactly what details mark a distinct type.[1] This confusion was caused primarily because the coins under study were not dated and the exact context of the different portraits was not known. Die analysis has largely solved this problem; most portrait types are seen to cluster closely together in the linked sequence, making it easy to distinguish each from the others and also making it possible to identify variants with confidence.

FAUSTINA'S FIRST NUMISMATIC PORTRAIT

The die analysis allows us to pinpoint with confidence the very first replicas of Faustina's earliest known portrait type produced in the Roman mint. *Aureus* dies fa3 (Fig. 2.4) and fa9 (Fig. 6.1) can be identified from their position at the very beginning of the die-link chart (Fig. 2.1) as the first *aureus* dies cut for Faustina's gold coinage. This places these two replicas in closest proximity to the model (in whatever form that existed) and, in theory, makes these dies most likely to be faithful copies of it. And so in fact it appears they are. The rendering of the hair has a distinct plasticity; compared to dies that come later, the locks of hair are rounded and full rather than linear and flat. The quality of the engraving is very high and Faustina's hair is represented in careful detail. It is also clear that the engraver of these two dies comprehended her actual coiffure. The clearest manifestation of this is that the engraver appears to have observed that the bangs are woven into the braid (that is, the bangs consist of loops of hair that, at the end of their loop, are plaited to form the braid itself), even if the braid is rendered in a more linear fashion than is seen in sculpted portraits. Evidence of this detailed understanding of the actual structure of Faustina's hairdo quickly fades from the coinage (see below on variants).

1. Fittschen 1982, 36; Ameling 1992, 163.

These Type 1 dies clearly parallel the earliest sculpted images of Faustina, the best example of which is the Capitoline portrait on display in the Stanza degli Imperatori (Fig. 6.2). The basic concept of the hairstyle is that Faustina's hair is gathered into a number of long braids which are pulled to the back of her head where they are rolled up into a bun. Between forehead and ear her hair is gathered in three or four (depending on the portrait) "bangs" that are draped in a curve onto her forehead and then pulled up and woven into a single braid that runs to the back of her head. Behind the ear the hair is pulled up directly into this braid. On the top of her head, Faustina's hair is divided into three sections on each side and likewise pulled back into the bun (though we cannot see the braids). All these braids are secured in a small, low bun at the back of her head; from sculpted portraits we know that this bun is actually a hollow circle of braids and that the single side-braid wraps up to bind the bottom of it. The earliest obverse dies in the *aureus* chain, fa3 and fa9, reproduce these details more or less faithfully. Both dies exhibit four bangs, and die fa9 also shows a very small part of the first bang on the opposite side of the head, evidence that the engraver relied on a three-dimensional model.

DID FAUSTINA HAVE AN EARLIER PORTRAIT TYPE?

Some dies with Type 1 portraits show three rather than four bangs (e.g., fa15 in Fig. 6.27). This arrangement is also seen in at least three sculpted images, and Markus Trunk has suggested that they may represent an earlier portrait of Faustina, presumably the first ever made for her, created on the occasion of her marriage in AD 145.[2] Although Trunk stops short of renumbering Fittschen's types, he argues that the four-bang variant is either a modification of the three-bang original or an entirely new type. The numismatic evidence cannot resolve this question with certainty, but it does make clear that both versions, with three or four bangs, were in use at the same time. The fact that the four-bang version is the first in sequence (fa3 and fa9 both employ this version; see Fig 2.1) suggests the three-bang version is a simplification achieved by omitting one of the bangs. But this sort of simplification is not, as far as we know, a feature of three-dimensional portrait carving. A bust of Faustina with four bangs would not have been replicated to produce variants with three bangs. The question remains open.

VARIANTS RESTRICTED TO THE MINT: 1A AND 1B

Much clearer is the case of the first major change in Faustina's numismatic portraiture. Very shortly after her coinage begins, the obverse obverse dies begin to exhibit differences that indicate that the die engravers were no longer making reference to their original model. This may be what lies behind the reduction in bang count from four to three. These changes are characterized by a gradual departure from reality, by which I mean a representation that is physically possible in a genuine hairstyle made of the wearer's hair (there is no evidence in any of Faustina's portraits that she wore a wig). The first of these is the tendency (beginning

2. Trunk (1999) groups together three of Faustina's busts: one in the Galleria Colonna (Fittschen 1982, cat. no. 10), one in the Munich Glyptothek (Fittschen 1982, cat. no. 9), and one in the Vatican Museo Chiaramonti (Fittschen 1982, cat. no. 3). He views these as replicas of a lost original that was distinct from Fittschen's type 1.

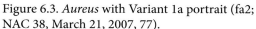

Figure 6.3. *Aureus* with Variant 1a portrait (fa2; NAC 38, March 21, 2007, 77).

Figure 6.4. *Aureus* with Variant 1b portrait (fa4; Rollin & Feuardent, 20–28, April 20, 1896, 416).

with die fa5—see Fig. 2.1) to depict the bangs in a tight S-curve, something that does not reflect the actual appearance of the known sculpted models and that is difficult to understand as a functional hairstyle. It appears that the die engravers, perhaps in the absence of a three-dimensional model, have begun to develop Faustina's portrait after their own fashion and after their own concept of how the hairstyle "works." Thus instead of reflecting the actual situation where locks of hair are bent in loops and then gathered up into a braid, the engravers have begun to imagine a situation where Faustina's hair cascades in waves *down* from the braid. This distinct change produces a clear variant (which I have called here Variant 1a, Fig. 6.3).

The second variant of Type 1 (Variant 1b) appears with the trio of dies fa11, 12, and 23 (Fig. 2.8). Its origins can already be seen in Variant 1a (e.g., die fa14 one link earlier, with larger image in Fig. 6.27), where the hair behind the ear is executed in simple curved lines and the bun-binding braid has become detached from the main braid around the forehead (of which, in sculptural representations, it is actually a part). This is Fittschen's type 2, but the evidence of die links suggests that it is not an independent type at all, rather a variant that evolved within the mint. With die fa11 and its companions (Fig. 2.8) we see a simplified rendering of Faustina's Type 1 portrait. The bangs have become rows of curved lines; the main braid is now a detached ornamental line, no longer linking up to the bun. The hair above this line, rather than being gathered into distinct rows, is now a series of simple lines moving from the crown of the head towards Faustina's face. The bun, now larger, sits higher on the head and is joined by three curving braids at the back. Although the overall shape of the Type 1 portrait remains, the details are all simplified and the components of the hairstyle no longer relate logically to each other. It is the only major and common numismatic portrait "type" of Faustina that does not have a parallel in sculpture; Fittschen argued that this is most likely because of a gap in our surviving evidence, not because such a sculpture was never created.[3] The die-link

---

3. Fittschen 1982, 48. Fittschen (personal correspondence) has also suggested to me that the locks with curved lines seen in this portrait have parallels in a Hadrianic portrait in the Capitoline Museum (Fittschen and Zanker 1983, no. 85, pp. 63–65, pl. 107). The locks in this portrait are smaller (seven to a side) and emerge from the bottom edge of a high nest. The

evidence, however, suggests that the change from Type 1 to first Variant 1a and then Variant 1b was the result of considerations specific to the medium of coinage, and especially to the small dies used to strike gold and silver, since Variant 1b is very rare on the bronze.

A number of factors probably contributed to this change. One is the obvious ease of execution brought by the simplification of the complicated Type 1 design; it would have been quicker to produce dies bearing Variant 1b portraits. The relatively quick but clearly sequential manner in which Variant 1b developed also suggests another probable contributing factor: that the model on which the portrait was based had been removed from the mint. If this happened at a relatively early time in the production of Faustina's coinage, the workers (as yet relatively unpracticed in executing her likeness) would have only been able to rely on previously produced coins for guidance. If the die engravers were working from other coins as models, it would have been easy to misunderstand or overlook the various components of the complicated hairstyle. The engravers' lack of experience may also have caused the only aspect of this variant that is a complication rather than a simplification: the addition of one or two extra braids behind the bun in Variant 1b. This feature, unknown on any three-dimensional portrait and also illogical, may have been influenced by the contemporary portraits of Diva Faustina, whose coins the mint was still producing. The elder Faustina's portraits involved a large bun and a series of braids that curve up the back of the empress's head, which may have inspired the additions to her daughter's portrait. This error remained uncorrected in the absence of the original model.

It is remarkable how much care was taken to cut dies bearing the unrealistic Variant 1b. Die fa4 (Fig. 6.4) exhibits a particularly fine style, with carefully rendered facial features and a high degree of detail in the hair, especially visible in the bun. Special care has been taken in the production of this die, but because it has all the unrealistic errors of this Variant in it shows that no three-dimensional Type 1 portrait remained for the engravers to copy. Type 1 variants had now assumed lives of their own in the mint.

Portrait Type 2

The first new type that reflects a genuine change in Faustina's appearance is manifested in Type 2. From a technical point of view, this Type is problematic. It exists in sculpture but is rare; Fittschen catalogues only two examples, both from Rome (Fig. 6.5).[4] On the other hand, it is relatively common on coins and shows two variants to the main type. The original Type 2 (that is, Type 2 when it first appears in the die link sequence; Fig. 6.6 and Fig. 3.6) has a high rigid bun and a single wave of hair at Faustina's brow. This main numismatic portrait corresponds most closely to the few known sculpted busts of this type. Numismatic Variant 2a (Fig. 6.7) has a low, loose bun and a double forehead wave; and 2b (Fig. 6.8) has a low, loose bun and a single forehead wave. The few known sculpted busts of this type correspond most closely to the main numismatic portrait Type 2, with its higher, rigid bun and single

hairstyle is unparalleled in the second century and it is, like Faustina's Type 1 variant, difficult to understand how it would have been created in reality. There are not to my knowledge any similar locks in the private portraiture of the Antonine period.

4. Fittschen 1982, 48–49.

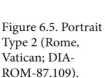

Figure 6.5. Portrait Type 2 (Rome, Vatican; DIA-ROM-87.109).

Figure 6.6. Type 2 (fd15; ANS 1955.191.15).

Figure 6.7. Variant 2a (fa7; ANS 1956.184.56).

Figure 6.8. Variant 2b (fd11; ANS 1958.223.4).

forehead wave. The not uncommon Variant 2a, with its double-wave of hair on the forehead, is unknown in sculpture. The more common Variant 2b is used on 26 obverse dies that likely represent a substantial period, perhaps a number of years, of coin production. But its low, loose bun appears to have no direct parallels in sculpture.

There are a number of possible interpretations of these variants. One is that, as with Type 1's variants, they were developed independently in the mint and do not necessarily reflect the actual appearance of Faustina. This seems unlikely. The development of Variants 1a and 1b was most likely brought about by two factors: a desire to simplify the execution of the complicated Type 1 portrait, and (this is connected to the first factor) confusion as to how exactly the hair arrangement functioned in real life. This resulted in the creation of portraits that were both geometrically abstracted and unrelated to actual practicalities of hair arrangement. Variants 2a and 2b do not exhibit these characteristics. If anything, they are more natural in appearance than the somewhat rigid Type 2 portraits, which share some of the characteristics of the late, abstract Variant 1b. And in Variants 2a and 2b the realistic depiction of the hair arrangement is never abandoned; it seems clear that the die engravers understood exactly how the brow wave was collected into a braid and then gathered with the rest of the hair in the bun. The conclusion is that these variants reflect changes in Faustina's actual appearance, ones that were picked up by the mint, but not reflected in three-dimensional sculpture.

The Order of Types 2, 3, and 4

From the die links it is abundantly clear that there is not a simple progression through the variants of Type 2. The rare dies with the main Type 2 portraits (e.g., fa8) come first; they are linked to the old Venus reverses used with Variant 1b dies. Variant 2a appears almost immediately (e.g., fa17 in Chain 2; Fig. 3.1). Variant 2b (including fd11 in Fig. 6.8) is in fact the latest portrait in the 2, 3, 4 sequence. It dominates Chain 3 (Fig. 3.7) and links directly to dies bearing the later portrait Type 5 (e.g., fd3) and the later reverse type of Venus (e.g., VB6). Types 3 and 4 belong *between* Variant 2a and Variant 2b. So the sequence is:

Figure 6.9. Type 3 portrait (Athens, National Museum; author).

Figure 6.10. Type 3 *aureus* (fd4; ANS 1944.100.81375).

Type 2, Variant 2a
Type 3
Type 4
Variant 2b
Type 5

Types 3 and 4

Type 3 portraits are similarly uncommon in both sculpture and coinage. Fittschen (who labels this his fourth type) suggests two examples from Rome that may be candidates, though both have highly-stacked buns, more reminiscent of Faustina the Elder.[5] A closer parallel comes from Athens (Fig. 6.9); it has a lower, though still fairly rigid bun. Both stone and coin versions of this portrait share the full-head wave pattern and a small projection of hair in front of the ear.

The Type 4 portrait appears only on one *aureus* die, fd14 (Fig. 6.11 and Fig. 3.7), but it is relatively common on medallions (Fig. 6.12; a medallion is a large coin-like object, struck from dies but normally larger and heavier than a coin). Three of the total 11 known medallion dies of Faustina catalogued by Mittag bear portrait Type 4 and in each case the legend on the medallion is exactly the same as on the single *aureus* die bearing the Type 4 portrait. The medallion reverses depict either a peacock with tail spread (Fig. 6.12) or, as is known from only one example, a complicated type showing Venus and cupids.[6] Remarkably, given the rarity of the type on coinage, there is a possible sculptural parallel for the otherwise rare

5. Fittschen 1982, 49–50 and pls. 17–18.
6. Mittag 2019, cat. nos. 277 (Venus), 279 (large medallion with peacock; Mittag lists three examples of this medallion, which weigh between 37 and 47 g, about double the weight of a normal *sestertius*) and 280 (small medallion with peacock, two examples ca. 15 g each); Gnecchi 1912, 42, Faustina 35, pl. 69.10.

Figure 6.11. Type 4 on an *aureus* (fd14; ANS 2017.34.1).

Figure 6.12. Type 4 on a bronze medallion (after Gnecchi 1912, pl. 69.10).

Figure 6.13. Type 4 portrait (Athens, Acropolis Museum, after Stavridis 1987, pl. 91).

Figure 6.14. Type 5 *aureus* (fd1; ANS 1958.223.5).   Figure 6.15. Type 5 portrait (Vatican, Galleria
                                                               Chiaramonti, inv. 1676; DAI-ROM-87 Vat.247).

portrait Type 4 in a recently published bust in the Acropolis museum (Fig. 6.13; it was found entangled in the roots of a tree in the Agora). The bun is larger than that shown on the *aureus* and medallion dies and the waves on the top of Faustina's head are not as pronounced, but the overall hairstyle is very similar. In the original publication of the head, Alkmini Stavridis identified the portrait as Faustina based on the close similarity between its facial features and those of two more certain portraits of her in the Athens National Museum; Ameling accepted the identification.[7] Stavridis does not offer an interpretation of the divergent coiffure, except to note the high quality of the work and to remark that the carver "chose a different hairstyle."[8] The identification of this portrait type on one coin and one medallion die lends strong support to its identification as Faustina.

PORTRAIT TYPE 5

Type 5, with Faustina's hair pulled back into a small low bun, represents a great simplification of her hairstyle. At least six sculpted replicas of Portrait Type 5 are known, though their identification is complicated because Faustina's daughter Lucilla was also depicted with this hairstyle.[9] From a technical point of view a major discrepancy between sculpted and numismatic portraits of this type can be seen in Faustina's bun. On almost all coins it is shown as a small, coiled nest of braids projecting significantly from the back of the head; sometimes a number of small "balls" appear at the apex of the bun (Fig. 6.14). In sculpture

7. Stavridis 1987, 107–108 for the identification. Ameling (1992, 149, n. 10) accepts the identification as Faustina the Younger.
8. Stavridis 1987, 108. The article in which the portrait is published is brief, only two pages in length.
9. Fittschen 1982, 51–52.

Figure 6.16. *Sestertius* with variant of Type 5 portrait (*BMCRE* Pius 2184).

on the other hand the bun has a flatter profile and lacks the "balls" so often seen on the coins (Fig. 6.15). The bun itself often appears to be conceived as woven locks of hair, rather than coiled ones, as seen on most coin dies (the bun in Fig. 6.15 has not been completely carved), and this corresponds to Janet Stephens's experimental reconstruction of the hairstyle.[10] When viewed from the back (e.g., Fittschen 1982, pl. 19), some of these sculpted portraits show the interwoven braid, and these shapes can appear like low lumps; these might be the origin of the "balls" seen on some of the numismatic versions of this type, but they are almost invisible in side-views of the sculpture.

The single exception to this puzzling discrepancy is a *sestertius* in the British Museum (Fig. 6.16) that bears an otherwise unique variant of the Type 5 numismatic portrait: the bun at the back of Faustina's head is not the small, coiled nest as on all other Type 5 coin portraits, but rather is low, elongated, and clearly braided. That is to say, it reflects exactly the appearance of the bun we see on sculpted portraits of Faustina. The detail of the braiding and the proportions of the bun to the head indicate that the die engraver had access to a sculpted Type 5 portrait as a model. It is difficult to say why this manner of engraving Faustina's bun was not carried out on other obverse dies with Type 5 portraits. Possibly the cutting of the braiding of the bun, with its rectilinear shapes intersecting at right (or near-right) angles, was too difficult and time-consuming, or too prone to error (such as through slippage of the engraving tool), to employ in normal die engraving for this portrait type.

Sculpted Replicas of Portrait Type 6

The dramatic Type 6 is difficult to understand as it is shown on coins (Fig. 6.17, minted under Marcus Aurelius, and Fig. 6.18, minted under Antoninus Pius). The hair is gathered in a bun as on Type 5, but the head does not show strands or braids pulled to the back.

10. Stephens 2008, fig. 6.

Figure 6.17. *Aureus* with Type 6 portrait (fm20; Vienna 36789 = 122874).

Figure 6.18. *Aureus* with Type 6 portrait (ff12; ANS 1958.223.8).

Figure 6.19. Portrait Type 6 (Athens, National Museum, DAI-Z-NEG-11397).

Figure 6.20. As 6.19, three-quarter view (DAI-Z-NEG-11378).

Instead the main feature is a series of wavy lines arranged in parallel rows, each rendered in unbroken engraving. The spaces between the curves of these lines are larger near the top of the head and become narrower around the face. It is hard to comprehend from the coins how such a hair arrangement would have worked in practice. But it does seem clear that we cannot be dealing with a case of transformation by the die-engravers of a real hairstyle into an unreal variant. There is, fortunately, a sculptural type that has a strong resemblance to Type 6 as seen on coins.[11] Fittschen, as variant B of his type seven, recognized one portrait originally identified by Wegner in the Athens National Museum (Fig. 6.19) and added further examples from Marathon, Bucharest, Rome, and Sperlonga.[12]

These sculptures show Faustina's hair divided into six waves on each side of the head, the upper four broad but the one nearest the face narrow; the hair in the bottom waves appears in places to intertwine, especially when viewed from the front (Fig. 6.20). This style is highly complicated, so much so that it is easy to imagine a die-engraver adopting a graphic shortcut to render it more easily. The feature he decided to copy was the tightening of the waves of hair close to the face; in doing so, he sacrificed the division of the hair into three waves that can be seen on the sculpture.

The die links (Chains 5 and 6, see Fig. 4.2) make it clear that portrait Types 5 and 6 were used at the same time. What is more, Type 5 is used exclusively in Chain 5, Type 6 exclusively in Chain 6. The contemporary nature of these chains is conclusively demonstrated by the fact that each documents the exact point when Faustina's filiation is dropped from the coinage. That is to say, the dies in both independent chains must have been in use at the time when it was decided to remove the filiation. This is clear evidence of a division of production in the mint. Portrait Type 6 does not outlive Type 5. Group 12 (Fig. 4.4), where portrait Type 5 and 6 are both used with a new reverse type of Juno, documents the abolishment of whatever mint division had created the parallel Chains 5 and 6. Thereafter only Type 5 was used (Pairs 9–12 in Die Chart 5 and Group 13 in Fig. 4.4, with the new reverse type of Fecunditas with four children) until the new Type 7 portrait was introduced. From this one may conclude that Type 5 was no longer current (that is to say, that Faustina no longer wore her hair in that style; this would agree with the relative uncommonness of the type in sculpture), but that it was employed alongside Type 6 in the mint for a reason that concerned the mint's own internal workings. This might have been the assignment of a specific engraver to each workshop, one of whom was not trained in the execution of the new portrait type, or to which workshop the information about the new type was not passed through an oversight.

FAUSTINA'S LATER PORTRAITS

Types 7, 8, and 9 initially overlapped; in other words, they were used at roughly the same time in the mint. I have numbered these portrait types in an order that reflects their "peak" popularity in the mint relative to each other. It is not clear from the die links which type appeared first, but Type 9 is entirely dominant in the later part of the die-link chain (Fig. 4.9). Type 9 is also the most common of all of Faustina's portrait types in sculpture. Fittschen catalogued 21 examples (not including six that he classified as variants, but which in fact belong to the earlier portrait Type 6).[13] Five of these portrait heads are veiled, which Fittschen interprets as an indicator that they are posthumous. The coinage on the other hand only

11. Fittschen 1982, 58–59. He treats this type as a variant of numismatic Type 9, with four or more parallel waves of hair gathered into a bun, but from the die analysis it is clear that Type 9 is significantly later than Type 6.

12. Wegner 1939, pl. 38; Fittschen 1982, pl. 34.

13. Fittschen 1982, 55–57.

Figure 6.21. Type 7 *aureus* (fm74; *BMCRE* Marcus 153).

Figure 6.22. Type 7 portrait (Rome, Museo Nazionale delle Terme, inv. 642; DAI-ROM-38.740).

Figure 6.23. Type 9 *aureus* (fm14; ANS 1944.100.49230).

Figure 6.24. Type 9 portrait (Rome, Capitoline Museum, inv. 250; DAI-ROM-57.746 OR Fittschen??).

Figure 6.25. Type 10 *aureus* (fm44; ANS 1959.228.3).

Figure 6.26. Type 10 portrait (Rome, Capitoline Museum, inv. 310; DAI-ROM-4379).

depicts Type 10 portraits of Faustina on her posthumous issues, suggesting (though not proving) that the veiled Type 9 portraits have another purpose. Veiling may indicate the wearer's participation in a sacrifice, as seen for example in the figure pouring a libation over an altar on the reverse of the Mater Castrorum type (see Fig. 4.12). Comparisons of sculpted and numismatic portraits for Types 7, 9, and 10 are given below; for Type 8, which is rare in sculpture, it has not been possible to find a suitable image; at any rate, both versions (sculpted and numismatic) are essentially identical to Type 7 but without the braid.

SUMMARY

Die analysis of Faustina's gold coinage shows that ten distinct portrait types were employed in the mint, along with at least six major variants of these main types. The analysis shows that one of Fittschen's nine types (his second type, here Variant 1b) was not a genuine stand-alone type but rather a variant created in the mint, brought about through a process of simplification and abstraction in the absence of a model. The analysis also shows that two new types must be added to the repertoire of Faustina's portraiture: the rare Type 4 (known only from one *aureus* and one medallion die) and the more common Type 6 (grouped by Fittschen as a variant of his seventh type, but shown by die analysis to be chronologically distinct). Both Types 4 and 6 find parallels in sculpture. The following chapter addresses the question of why these various portrait types were created, and what they meant.

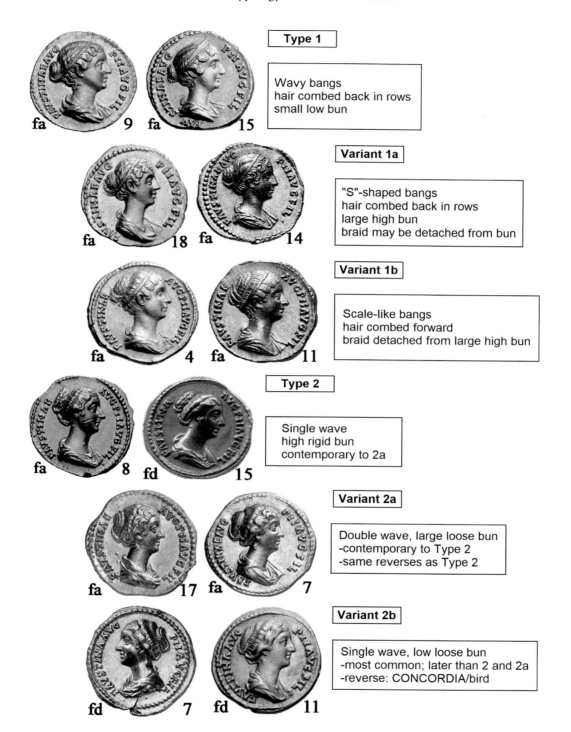

Figure 6.27. Faustina's numismatic portrait types in chronological order.

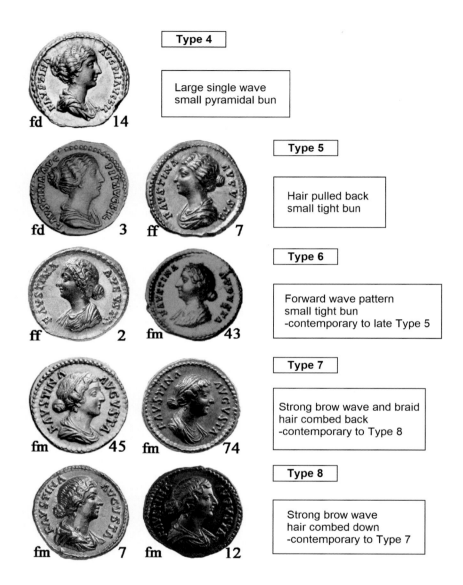

Figure 6.28. Faustina's numismatic portrait types in chronological order (continued).

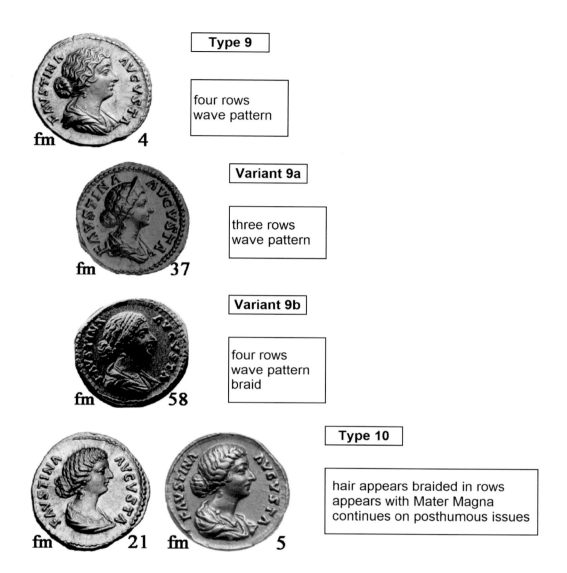

Figure 6.29. Faustina's numismatic portrait types in chronological order (continued).

Chapter 7
Message and Meaning in the Portraits of Faustina

The interpretation of Faustina's portraits changed significantly over the course of the twentieth century. Writing in the 1930s, Wegner was quick to find evidence in Faustina's portrait of her character. With reference to her appearance after Marcus succeeded Pius to the throne, he wrote that "a dull but uppity look and an enchanting mouth betray the character of an ignoble woman of few accomplishments, who was notorious for her immoral lifestyle."[1] In the case of Type 9 Wegner noted that Faustina's facial characteristics appear older. "The cheeks are tight and less full; the chin thus gives the impression of being pointier. Unstable, devious character is concealed in the expression of the wandering gaze and closed lips."[2] These judgments are based, of course, on the portrayal of Faustina in Cassius Dio and the *Historia Augusta* and are a good illustration of the tendency in early portrait scholarship to look for evidence of the character of a person in their portraits.[3] Wegner's subjective and superficial judgement of Faustina's portraits also reveals a double standard in his treatment of men and women. For the former, Wegner advanced the then-novel theory that new portrait types were created for special events in an emperor's life, but for the imperial women, he viewed their multiple portrait types as simple manifestations of fickle fashion.

Modern scholarship has extended the theory of event-triggered portrait type change to the imperial women. Fittschen, in his 1982 monograph that extensively utilized the numismatic evidence, made the bold hypothesis that Faustina's many types were created to mark the births of her many children. Fittschen criticized earlier research that treated Faustina's multiple

1. Wegner 1939, 53. "Ein dummdreister Blick und ein liebreizender Mund verraten den Charakter einer unedlen, wenig ausgezeichneten Frau, die wegen ihres sittenlosen Lebenswandels beruechtigt war."
2. Wegner 1939, 54. "Die Wangen sind straffer und weniger voll gebildet; das Kinn wirkt dadurch noch etwas spitzer. Unstetes, unaufrichtiges Wesen verbirgt sich im Ausdruck des abirrenden Blickes und der verschlossenen Lippen."
3. On the error of reading personality from ancient portraits in the cases of Caracalla and Nero, see Davies 2007, 312–315.

portrait types as little more than "a useful illustration of the development of female hairstyles" and defined the goal of his work as "to show that the portraits of the empress were in no way a fashionable game, but that their creation was due to very specific occasions and therefore were intended to fulfil concrete functions."[4] In a nutshell, Fittschen's thesis is that each new type (defined primarily by a new arrangement of the hair) was created when Faustina gave birth to a child (or children, in the case of twins).

While Fittschen's typology has come to be generally accepted, his thesis about the reason behind the many changes in portrait type has met with a mixed response. The most thorough critique was made by Ameling in 1992, who began with a detailed investigation of the evidence for the children of Faustina and Marcus, which he pared down to 9 from the 11 proposed by Fittschen. Ameling then proceeded to evaluate Fittschen's thesis by trying to determine whether or not each of the portrait type changes could be associated with evidence of a new birth in terms of coin types (that is, following Fittschen's own methodology). He made the very important observation that Fittschen's thesis would work only under the assumption that a coin with birth iconography and a given portrait type would also be the earliest coin to bear that portrait type. This, Ameling noted, could only be proven by a more detailed study. Also problematic is the fact that some births in Fittschen's list (a boy in 157/8 and a girl in the 160s) do not have a new portrait type associated with them. Alexandridis concluded in 2004 that while Fittschen's work doubtlessly points in the right direction by emphasizing the importance of the imperial progeny under the Antonines, the arguments used to associate every portrait change with a new birth are often built on tenuous evidence; Barbara Levick in 2014 called Fittschen's hypothesis "implausible," and asserted that "some births, such as that of Annia Galeria Aurelia Faustina in 151, had no impact on the coinage."[5] R. R. R. Smith in his 1983 review of Fittschen concluded that his theory "must be roughly right" but expressed some reservations, among them our lack of knowledge as to why exactly portrait types were created and some uncertainty about the relationship between numismatic portraits and those in other media.[6] Fittschen responded to criticism of his theory by reiterating that "in several cases it is unmistakably clear that the change in hairstyle is linked up with the birth of a child to Faustina." He added that it is not possible "to make progress by casting doubt on the correctness of this thesis without providing any necessary reasons or presenting more plausible alternatives."[7]

The die analysis presented here allows Fittschen's theory to be tested by detailed observation of portrait change in the iconographic context provided by the sequence of reverse types. But the die analysis also offers more opportunities to explore the meaning of Faustina's portrait types. Chief among these are the chance to observe in exact detail the precise working of the mint when creating portraits, and, more broadly, to assess and critique some of the concepts

4. Wegner 1939, 18. Fittschen (1982, 19, n. 19) supported this assertion with reference to Zanker's 1978 work on the Actium type of Augustus and Bergmann's 1978 work on Marcus Aurelius.

5. Ameling 1992, 165–166; Alexandridis 2004; Levick 2014, 95; on the reasons for changes in portraiture Levick cites "annual or one-off celebrations" but does not reference evidence. Others, e.g., Mikocki (1995, 63), accept Fittschen's theory without discussion ("on peut classer les portraits de Faustine suivant la naissance des nombreux enfants successifs").

6. Smith 1983, 229.

7. Fittschen 2010, 231.

and theories on which the study of Roman portraiture is based, especially the concept of the type and the theories behind type creation.

THE INTERPRETATION OF PORTRAIT TYPES

There is no disagreement among scholars about the existence of portrait types in ancient Rome. The exact replication of specific details, especially of the hair, on sculpted heads found in different provinces of the empire makes clear that distinct portrait models existed, and that these were copied with great care. The problem lies in the interpretation of the types. New portrait types of emperors and empresses are generally thought to have been created for important occasions, including "the assumption of important offices (e.g., the consulate), the bestowal of particular titles (e.g., "Augustus," *pater patriae*, etc.), military victories, and imperial anniversaries".[8] Fittschen suggested in 1999 that Marcus Aurelius had new types created on this occasion of his being named Caesar and for his first consulate and that Commodus had a type created when named *princeps iuventutis*.[9] In Fittschen's opinion it is "entirely legitimate to apply this model in the other, remaining cases," though he cautiously notes that "the evidence is often ambiguous" and that theories derived from this model "cannot be understood as established facts but rather as suggestions only."[10] A notable situation in which such theories should be applied with care is the depiction of the aging of a subject. This is especially true for those who were portrayed first as boys or young men, such as Nero or Commodus. Marianne Bergmann has closely considered the effects of aging on the portraits of Marcus Aurelius and proposed that "versions" of his main portraits types were created as the emperor aged, especially for his type II portrait; she places the many known examples in order based on beard length as reflected on coins.[11]

While aging is certainly evident over the long course of Faustina's portrait development, the changes that are seen in hair arrangement and their faithful replication in sculpted portraits found all over the Roman empire conform precisely with the traditional definition of typological change. So the question is, why in the case of Faustina were these different types created? Fittschen's argument rests on the prevalent theory (seldom explicitly stated, but observable in many discussions of portrait type change) that a portrait type was the equivalent of a special honour created for an emperor (or empress) on a noteworthy occasion. This concept is so well established that even Fittschen's critics have held to it.[12] But there have been some exceptions. Smith, although following the accepted theory for sculpted portraits, allowed for the possibility that the mint may have handled portraiture differently than the sculptural workshop. He suggested that "[i]t is possible that some variations in image, like

8. Fittschen 2010, 228.
9. Fittschen 1999, 31, 62.
10. Fittschen 2010, 229.
11. Bergmann 1978, 40–41.
12. E.g., Alexandridis 2004, 29: "Im Leben einer Kaiserin gab es noch andere Ereignisse, die eines neuen Bildnisses würdig sein konnten, wie z.B. Hochzeit, Ernennung zur Augusta oder andere Ehrungen (bei Faustina eventuell die Ernennng zur *mater castrorum*), eventuell auch der Regierungsantritt des Mannes." Similarly Smith (1983, 229): "Portraits mediated the imperial family to the empire and new types were probably therefore connected with dynastic events: conferring of titles, adoptions, marriages, apotheoses, and the like."

small hairstyle changes, could have been put through the mints more easily, and might not have been considered sufficiently important to be put through what must have been the less agile machinery for the distribution of types in the round. Alternatively, such variations could merely have originated in and stayed within the mints; in this case one should be careful in the classification of official portrait types as against variants."[13] And more recently, in 1998, Jane Fejfer challenged the basic idea of a connection between the creation of a type and specific events and has argued that new types might have resulted from competition between different workshops, in "a flexible system where ideological concerns in the styling of the portrait type, its interaction with portraits of private citizens, its ideological and technical successes, demands for renewal, and marketing mechanisms, all influenced the concept of imperial portraits."[14] The lack of evidence for the traditionally suggested occasions for portrait type creation has been pointed out by Jakob Højte in his study of Roman Imperial statue bases from around the empire.[15] He found no evidence in them that the sort of special occasions normally supposed by portrait scholars actually led to the erection of portrait statues. His conclusions have been challenged by Kropp and by Christopher Hallett, who point out that (as Højte himself acknowledges) the preserved bases and preserved portraits are not drawn from the same pool and are unlikely to be directly comparable (the portraits are primarily from Italy and many probably from private contexts, while most bases come from the provinces and probably supported bronze statues).[16] Nonetheless, Højte's analysis does make clear the weak evidentiary basis for the event-associated theory of portrait type creation. Here the coinage can make a useful contribution.

COINS, PORTRAITS, AND MEANING

Because we have no explicit ancient evidence to help us answer the question of why new portrait types of Roman emperors and empresses were created, everything we know must be extracted from study of the portraits and their context.[17] In this area coinage has traditionally played an auxiliary role, helping to identify portraits but doing little more. There are some exceptions. Coins provide the best evidence for the date of Augustus's Prima Porta type, and for the reasons behind its creation. This type made its first appearance on *cistophori* of Pergamum or Ephesus dated to 27–25 BC; these same coins also bear for the first time the emperor's new title Augustus.[18] This is strong evidence that the new portrait type was created at this time; or at least, that a statue of the emperor was erected at about this time, perhaps as part of the honors voted to Augustus together with his new name in 27 BC, the portrait head of which became the model for many other likenesses of him throughout the empire. The

13. Smith 1983, 229.
14. Fejfer 1998, 47 and 2008, 419 (source of quotation).
15. Højte 2005.
16. Kropp 2008, Hallett 2007.
17. On the lack of ancient evidence for portrait type creation, see Ameling 1992, 148.
18. Zanker 1978, 44, n. 120. The coins in question are the *cistophori* of Sutherland's small Group II: Sutherland 1970, 14–16 and pl. 2. On the high degree of accuracy in the replication of the type, see Boschung 1993, 61.

crucial factor here is the precise dating of the coinage, which allows the portrait, in turn, to be placed in its historical context.

The multiplicity of Faustina's portrait types requires great precision from the coin evidence if it is to make a genuine contribution to their interpretation. Fortunately this is exactly what the results of the die analysis provide, in many cases at least. Die analysis not only supplies the sequence of types and a solid relative (and sometimes precise absolute) dating, but also contextualizes the portraits firmly in the developing iconography of the reverses. This is perhaps the single most important contribution of die analysis to the study of Faustina's portraits, because it gives us the opportunity to observe, in the form of the iconography and epigraphy of the reverses of the coinage, the ideological context of new portrait types at the time of their creation. The results can also be used to critique the theories on which the study of Roman portraits in general is based, especially the concept of type and its interpretation, and to propose new theories to explain what is seen in the numismatic evidence. These are exactly the circumstances that are proposed by Ameling as necessary for understanding what portraits meant: "If on the other hand a sequence of types is accurately dated, then it is possible to search for connections with other events, for causes and correspondences—from which one might perhaps come to a well-founded hypothesis of the reasons for type change."[19]

Despite the great detail offered by the results of the die analysis, the interpretation that follows still requires some assumptions. The most important of these is that both the portrait and reverse types seen in the die analysis of Faustina's gold coinage represent their first appearances. In the absence of evidence otherwise, if the precise point in the die link sequence when a type first appears on the *aurei* can be determined, I treat that as evidence of the point of creation of the type. There is no evidence in the silver and bronze coinage of portrait types appearing earlier than on the gold; there is, however, some rare evidence of reverse types appearing on silver or bronze coins before they appear on the gold (Hilaritas is a good example). In these situations I have been careful to note them. There is also something that I do not assume: a common origin of numismatic and sculpted portrait types, even if it is clear that these are very closely related (as shown by the striking correspondence in form between the two genres, in most cases). The die analysis has already shown that portraits could behave differently in the mint than they did in their three-dimensional incarnations, in the form of the variants of Portrait Type 1. If such variation could happen in the mint, it is possible that there are other significant differences between the portrait type repertoires in the different media.

VARIATIONS BETWEEN MEDIA

The most important difference between portraits in the two main media (sculpture and coins) has to do with their relative numbers, both within media (between the different metals on the coinage) and between media (sculpture versus coins). To begin with the coinage, gold has the

19. Ameling 1992, 148. "Ist eine Reihe von Typen dagegen genau datiert, so kann nach Verknüpfungen mit anderen Ereignissen, nach Ursachen und Zusammenhängen gesucht werden - wodurch man eventuell zu einer begründeten Hypothese für die Gründe des Typenwechsels gelangen kann."

Table 7.1. Direct comparison between the numbers of dies used for the gold coinage for each portrait type and the number of examples of sculptures in the round that are known for each type.

Coin Portrait Type	Fittschen Type	# *Aureus* Dies	# Sculpted Portraits
1	1 and 2	20	10
2	3	27	2
3	4	4	3
4	-	1	1
5	5	30	6
6	7b	10	6
7	8	5	15
8	6	4	3
9	7	24	21
10	9	9	2
		132	69

widest range (and the only full range) of portraits. Type 4 is entirely absent on the normal silver and bronze coinage but is relatively common on medallions; Type 2 only appears in its variants on the other metals; Type 3 is very rare on silver and bronze. The most probable factor to account for this is chronological: if gold was produced more or less constantly, but silver and bronze only at intervals, this could have led to differences in portraits employed simply based on which ones were current when the silver and bronze were struck. The differences in the employment of portrait types between the media of coins and sculpture are equally striking.

Table 7.1 presents a direct comparison between the numbers of dies used for the gold coinage for each portrait type and the number of examples of sculptures in the round that are known for each type. It is immediately evident that while there are some close correspondences (especially the nearly-equal proportions of Type 1 *aureus* dies and sculpture), there are also dramatic differences between the two media. Part of this may be due to the chance of preservation, particularly since in the case of coin dies we have a much greater mass of surviving material and in many cases more than one example (coins) of each replica (dies), while with sculpture we are reliant on the preservation of the individual replicas. But even if we accept that the surviving evidence may not completely reflect the actual situation in antiquity, there are some divergences that are simply too large to be explained by chance. Why, for example, are there so many surviving sculpted portraits of Type 7, when it was used for only a very short period on the coinage? Why, on the other hand, do Types 2 and 5 appear much more commonly on coins than in sculpture?

The reason almost certainly has to do with differences in the chronological patterns of replica creation in the two media, and in particular with greater variation over time in the creation of sculpted portraits. The (relatively) large numbers of Type 7 sculpted portraits surviving may be due to this having been the main current portrait type at the time when

Marcus Aurelius became emperor, following the death of his father Antoninus Pius. The accession of a new emperor to the throne is an indisputable occasion for the setting up of new statues and thus for the creation of new portraits (though this did not have to mean creation of new types). Faustina's status did not change—she remained, as before, Augusta—but her image may have been reproduced more frequently at this time if (as was common especially in the east) some of these new dedications were family groups. The relatively low frequency of Types 2 and 5 portraits in sculpture, on the other hand, suggests that after a spurt of early sculptural dedications (perhaps in 145 on the occasion of her marriage to Marcus), the pace slowed down; coinage however continued to be produced regularly.

COIN PORTRAIT CREATION IN CONTEXT

Why were Faustina's portrait types created? The context offered by die links, and especially by the newly established sequence of reverse types, offers some tentative answers. The numismatic evidence cannot tell us whether Type 1 was created at the same time that Faustina's coinage began celebrating of the birth of her first child (it may have already been in existence), but it does make clear that great care was taken in the engraving of the first two *aureus* dies with this type. Variants 1a and 1b, on the other hand, clearly have nothing to do with any outside events, but rather were more or less "natural" developments within the mint, created when the engravers continued their work without reference to a clear model. Type 2 coincides with a significant change in the iconography of the coinage, including the introduction of the type Juno with two children. The die links are fragmentary at the time Type 3 was initiated, and there is no clear indication that its occurrence coincided with any significant change in the reverse iconography. For the rare Type 4 we may make this statement absolutely: it appeared on the gold coinage without any change in the reverse typology.[20] Type 5 on the other hand is closely connected to a clear change in the epigraphy and iconography of the reverse: from CONCORDIA and a dove to VENVS and a figure of the goddess. But the type, Venus holding an apple and a staff, offers us no clear clues as to why it was introduced. Type 6 appears to coincide with the introduction of a new reverse type, Diana. This is again an unspecific iconographic reference, but there is a potentially significant epigraphic change: the shifting of Faustina's filiation to the reverse, leaving the obverse bearing the simple yet powerful title Faustina Augusta. At the same time, Type 5 does not disappear from the coinage but rather continues to be used in parallel, indicating that the production of gold coinage was at this time divided into two "streams" that did not share dies between them.

Then comes a remarkable and very informative change. Well documented by the particularly coherent parallel die chains (Fig. 4.2), we see dramatic shifts in iconography and epigraphy in both streams of production. First, Faustina's filiation disappears from the coinage. This coincides precisely with the introduction of two new coin types, one in each of the parallel streams, and these types entirely replace the old Diana reverse. One of the new

20. Though note that Type 4 also appears on bronze medallions. It is thought that such objects were created for distribution on special occasions, for example, at the New Year. This may indicate that Type 4 was connected to a special event, but we cannot be certain. On the occasions for the issue of medallions, see most recently Mittag 2012, 21–22 and 106–107.

types is Diana Lucifera, shown holding a torch; the other is Fecunditas, depicted with three children. The ideological message of the coinage is now modified, becoming sharply focused on the theme of childbirth. At the same time it is clear that there is no change in the portrait typology. Soon after, the die chains (which become more fragmentary) show that the two parallel streams of production have rejoined, and that portrait Type 6 has been abandoned in favor of the older Type 5, which had never gone out of use. Type 5 then continues on, through a major development in reverse typology: the appearance of four children in the "fruitfulness of the times" type and the depiction of the twins on their throne. Unfortunately the fragmentary nature of the die link chain at this point makes it hard to be certain whether or not Types 7, 8, and 9 are connected to a change in reverse typology. This does seem probable for Type 7, which is linked in its earliest appearance to Salus and, perhaps also early, to the type TEMPOR(um) FELIC(itas) showing six children. Portrait Type 10 appears exclusively with the reverses Cybele (MATRI MAGNAE), Venus Felix, and MATER CASTRORVM. The fact that none of these link to the earlier die chains suggests that these types represent a new issue after a period when no gold coinage was struck for Faustina.

What does all this mean for Fittschen's theory? The strongest conclusions may be drawn from the first portion of Faustina's coinage, which is to say up to and including Type 6 (reference in the following discussion to types are, as in the remainder of this work unless otherwise noted, to the new type numbers employed throughout this study). In this time period, the die link chains are more complete and we may be more certain of being able to observe the sequence of changes on both obverse and reverse in their original order. For Type 1, it is unclear whether or not it was an original creation. Type 2, on the other hand, certainly was, and it is associated with a new reverse indicating childbirth. Types 5 and 6 appear concurrent with a reverse type change that is *not* connected (at least, not in any clear way) to childbirth. And Types 3 and 4 do not appear to be related to any significant shift in reverse type or inscription. The results of this analysis show that Fittschen's theory does not apply in most cases, at least as far as we can judge from the evidence at hand.

A NEW THEORY OF PORTRAIT TYPE CREATION

The large number of sculpted portraits attested for Faustina the Younger sets the empress apart, in relative terms, from all other members of the imperial house, before and after (though Plautilla, wife of Caracalla, had more change in a shorter period of time; given the length of time over which Faustina was depicted, her likeness changed only every three years on average). The challenge has been to explain this variety within the accepted model of Roman portraiture creation, which asserts that new portrait types were created to mark special occasions in the life of an emperor or empress. This model has no definite ancient evidence to support it and, perhaps surprisingly, there has been little very little discussion until recently of the theory behind it. It appears that early scholars of Roman imperial portrait typology arrived at this model in a fairly direct manner; one wonders if they were influenced by the modern practice of having portraits, especially photographic ones, made on occasions of special personal significance. We do not know if, and if so to what degree, the Romans thought in this way about portraits and until recently very little thought has been given to other factors influencing the media by which portraits have been conveyed to us.

The existence of portrait types is beyond dispute, but we should seriously consider the possibility that the generally accepted model for their creation is wrong. To begin with, what a type requires to come into being is the creation of multiple copies based on a single model; there is no requirement that the model itself must have been created to mark a special occasion for the subject it depicts. Other possibilities are imaginable: that a particular statue was chosen for copying because it was especially esteemed, or just easily accessible; then this model was disseminated by a system, the exact workings of which we do not know (although we know much about the techniques of creating copies, we are in the dark when it comes to the system by which these were disseminated). Such a statue might well have been created to honor an emperor on a special occasion, or it might not. And this is all speculation anyhow. In some cases it is clear that imperial portraits are differentiated by the subject's age (Nero, for example, or Commodus). From the information available, it is not necessary to suggest anything more than that a new portrait was created when it was clear that the extant portrait no longer reflected the actual appearance of the emperor.

A theory based on the concept that portrait types were created mainly to keep the image of the emperor or empress current does not exclude the potential influence of ideological factors. When it was decided to create a new portrait, its appearance could have been influenced by a variety of factors, not least the subject him or herself. A person might manipulate aspects of their own appearance for specific purposes, for example Pompey's adoption of the anastole (recalling Alexander). The strength of this idea with respect to Faustina is that it not only effectively explains most of the changes in Faustina's portrait typology, but that it also might open up new approaches to our understanding of the self-representation of the empress. The mint operated in Rome, as close as it was possible to get to the center of imperial power. For the first fourteen years of production of Faustina's coinage the emperor, Antoninus Pius (and thus all the administrative and ceremonial machinery of the *aula*), was constantly in Rome or very near to it. The actual appearance of the empress could not have been unknown to the higher-ranked personnel in the mint, and more importantly the coins they produced would have come into the hands of thousands who knew this too. Let us assume that Faustina herself made changes in her personal appearance, at various times throughout her life and for different reasons, unknown to us. The mint, engaged in the (as far as we can tell) more or less constant production of coins bearing her image, would have had clear motivation to reflect these changes in the empress' appearance, if only for the sake of maintaining the validity of its product by accurately reflecting the imperial family member that gave it authority.

If we follow this alternate model there are interesting conclusions to be drawn. The most intriguing is that Faustina did at times orchestrate significant changes in her own appearance. The numismatic evidence shows that sometimes, early in her reign at least, these could coincide with the announcement of a new birth. At other times, they did not, and we must consider that the reasons for these changes may have been connected to factors that were unrelated to those that governed the change of reverse typology in the mint. The most probable factors of this class are ones connected to Faustina's role in imperial ceremonies.

We know little about her presence at court, but Cassius Dio (72.31.2) records among her posthumous honors "that a golden statue of Faustina should be carried in a chair into the theatre, on every occasion when the emperor was to be a spectator, and placed in the special section from which she herself had been wont, when alive, to view the games, and that the most influential women should sit round about it."[21] This gives us a glimpse of the public role played by the empress. If, during her lifetime, Faustina had been publicly surrounded by "the most influential women," this would have provided a context offering many opportunities for the manipulation of her self-image, a context in which the "influential women" would have been both audience (in addition to the broader public who would see Faustina and these attendants) and adjuncts (who by similarity or contrast in appearance would contribute to the effect, and presumably meaning, of the changes in Faustina's appearance).[22] A full investigation of the possible implications of this is beyond the scope of this study, but one observation can be made. In the Flavian period, as D'Ambra has shown, fashions in hair design were highly traditional and there is little evidence that the female members of the imperial family were trend setters; instead they represented themselves as traditional matrons and the iconography of their portraiture reflects and communicates this. In contrast, some of Faustina's hairstyles appear to be unparalleled in contemporary private portraiture.[23] This suggests that a different dynamic was at work in elite female self-representation in the Antonine period, one in which the empress did indeed play a leading role.

What does such a model imply for portrait production and typology outside the mint? It would be strange if the mint operated with a strong motivation to keep portrait appearance (= types) current, while the workshops creating three-dimensional (or painted) portraits did not. At least for workshops based in Rome, whose customers would presumably know (from coins if not from any other source) the actual appearance of the empress, the pressure to remain current in their depiction of members of the imperial family must have been substantial. But did these workshops have the same degree of flexibility in the handling of portrait types as we see in the mint? It is clear that the mint at times introduced a new portrait only to employ it for a short (sometimes very short) time, and then reverted to the production of an older portrait type. The fact that each of the types seen on coins, even the rare Type 4, also appear in sculpture suggests in fact that the sculptural workshops indeed were as flexible as the mint, at least to the extent that they also picked up these short-lived changes in Faustina's appearance. On the other hand, there are two characteristics of portrait type use in the mint that cannot be conclusively confirmed or denied in the case of sculptural workshops: the parallel employment of two different portrait types at one time, and the occasional re-introduction (normally one die only) of an earlier type in later production. The first phenomenon may indeed be determined by technical factors specific to the mint. When Types 5 and 6 were used in parallel, the production of aurei was divided into two workshops, which did not share dies (neither obverse nor reverse) between them. When this rigid workshop division vanished,

21. Dio 72.31.2, E. Carey trans.
22. On women and hair in Roman society, see especially D'Ambra 2013, Olson 2008, 70–76, and Bartman 2001.
23. D'Ambra 2013. For female portraits of the Antonine period, see Fittschen 1996, Fittschen and Zanker 1983. Many individual components of Faustina's portraits may be identified in private portraits, assembled into new styles.

Type 6 also vanished from the coins, suggesting that its use was connected in some way to the system of production employed. In the case of the rare later recurrences of earlier portrait types, it is conceivable that a mint engraver, perhaps returning to Faustina after a period engraving dies for Pius or Marcus, selected an incorrect model (presumably an earlier coin) to copy. This kind of error might also have occurred in sculptural workshops, especially in those far from Rome itself.

Conclusion

The traditional theory of portrait type creation finds little support in the evidence provided by the coinage issued in the name of Faustina the Younger. Only in the minority of cases are changes clearly connected to shifts in reverse typology that indicate significant events in her life (in these cases, childbirth). And in one case, such an event is clearly referenced while there is no change in the obverse portrait. This suggests that the traditional theory of portrait type creation is flawed and that a more probable theory must be proposed, at least in the case of Faustina, one based on a desire by the creators of portraits to remain current in their depictions of their subject. This returns some of the focus of portrait studies to the subject of the portrait and recalls the sometimes overlooked potential role played by the manipulation of personal appearance in day to day life by members of the Roman elite.

Conclusion

The Public Image of Faustina

From the beginning of Faustina's marriage to Marcus a definite change in the public image of the dynastic system can be discerned. While Nerva, Trajan, Hadrian, and Antoninus Pius had all adopted heirs (sometimes rather closely related ones), only Hadrian had announced his designated heirs (Aelius and Antoninus) extensively on coinage, and that only late in his reign.[1] Antoninus Pius likewise announced Marcus Caesar on his coinage. But in 147 we see the appearance of the image of Pius' young daughter Faustina on the obverses of the coinage, in the context of the birth of her daughter Domitia. This birth represented the first success of the newly-established dynastic system, triggering Faustina's promotion to Augusta and the initiation of coinage in her name while at the same time signalling the end of the adoptive tradition. Part of the role of the coinage was to make public the establishment of the new generation that would secure the leadership of the empire. Faustina's public role (at least as it was proclaimed on the coinage) was always first and foremost related to her being a mother; we see this beginning with the award of the title Augusta on the occasion of the birth of her first child.

The results of this study show that the exact manifestation of this role changed in important ways as time passed, and also that the nature of the dynastic system itself was changing. The die analysis makes it possible to perform an accurate comparison of the iconography of Faustina's coinage and the contemporary coinage of Antoninus Pius and Marcus Aurelius. This reveals a number of striking patterns in the division of commemoration of specific events in the imperial household—especially births of children—in unequal ways between Faustina and her father or her husband. The first birth is Faustina's alone, which is to say it is commemorated only

---

1. A rare *aureus* of Trajan (Woytek 2010, #582f) bears the portrait of Hadrian Caesar on the reverse. Only one die and two examples are known. The production of coinage under Hadrian for Aelius and Antoninus was much more extensive.

on her coinage, and no direct mention of it is made on the coinage of Marcus or Pius. Only three times (in 149, 160 and 161) is a birth commemorated simultaneously on the coinage of Faustina, Marcus, and Pius. And there is a long period between 149 and ca. 157 when there is very little evidence of any numismatic commemoration of an imperial birth by any member of the imperial family, although we know some children were born at this time (from their funerary inscriptions—see Appendix 1). These patterns indicate conscious decisions made to associate certain members of the imperial family with certain public messages and reveal that some messages were meant, at least from the evidence of the coinage, to be connected to Faustina alone. They also suggest that for about seven or eight years either interest in publicizing children on the coinage lapsed or no newly born child survived long enough to be so commemorated. I will return to this topic below.

The die analysis also makes clear that a new typology of Faustina's portrait types is required. These revisions do not turn the earlier typology on its head, but do require the removal a type identified by Fittschen, the addition of a new and until now unrecognized portrait type, and a reorganization of the order of some and the chronology of all of Faustina's portraits. Furthermore, the detailed information about the context of the use of different portrait types allows a number of important observations to be made as to exactly how they were employed in the mint. The patterns revealed are often complex and clearly do not follow a firm set of rules, a conclusion that cautions against the formulation of too-rigid theories of Roman portrait type creation and employment. Perhaps most importantly with regard to portraiture, the die study reveals the chronological sequence of the reverse iconography of Faustina's coinage *and* the exact relationship between this and the development of Faustina's portraiture. Thus it is possible to immediately evaluate the extant theories that have been proposed to explain the frequent changes in Faustina's portrait, and to suggest on the basis of the newly gained evidence a new and better-founded explanation for the phenomenon. Prominent here is Fittschen's theory that each new portrait was created to celebrate a new birth in the imperial family, but other theories have been suggested (and some older ones forgotten, perhaps unjustly). As with the sequence of portraits itself, the connections between change in obverse portrait and in reverse typology turn out not to follow one set rule. In only one case (portrait Type 2) is a connection to a birth in the imperial family absolutely clear, revealed by the synchronous appearance of a birth-associated reverse type and the new portrait type. Other obverse portraits, however, appear in the context of comparatively minor changes in reverse typology or are associated with no changes at all.

The evidence in fact points in a very different direction: to a situation where the mint at Rome often found itself reacting to changes in Faustina's appearance. This in turn means that we need to invert our concept of the creation of portrait types, for Faustina at least: they, the individual, distinct types, were not each created to honor Faustina; rather their creation was driven by Faustina herself, who changed her own appearance numerous times and who thus compelled the producers of portraits to keep up. Some of these changes she apparently orchestrated to coincide with the birth of a child; some she initiated at other times, for reasons we cannot know. One wonders if Faustina valued the diversity she injected into the growing body of portraits of herself. The sheer variety appears to be a novelty, but we must keep in mind that the time period in question is almost three decades. And whether Faustina was a unique agent of this trend, we also cannot know; her actions may reflect broader trends in female self-representation at the time. Certainly there are great differences in female portraiture in the Antonine period, including very many styles of hair arrangement that are never used by the empress. Of course she may not have cared what effect these changes in her appearance had on portraiture, as she may have orchestrated them for entirely unrelated reasons, ones to do perhaps with her self-representation in the context of the other women of the senatorial elite and her various appearances at court and in public.

Faustina, Pius, Marcus, and Fronto

I would like to conclude with an attempt to bring together the evidence of the iconography of Faustina's (and her father's and husband's) coinage and the only other major non-epigraphic contemporary source, the letters of Fronto, and to put this information in the context of the more commonly referenced literary sources, Cassius Dio and the *Historia Augusta*. Fronto was the tutor of Marcus Aurelius and a frequent correspondent, who left a collection of letters of great variety but the organization of which is sometimes less than clear.[2] Some scholars have supposed that Fronto was responsible for the editing of all the letters, but Edward Champlin favors the theory that he edited a few books during his lifetime, while the remainder were published after his death.[3] Whatever the case, we should consider these letters as at least in part consciously assembled, if not originally written, with an eye to the message that they would communicate to a future reader (other than the addressee). The earliest mention of Faustina, which occurs in a letter datable to the year 143, is a powerful reminder of this function of these supposedly private letters.[4] In it, Antoninus Pius thanks Fronto for a speech he gave in the Senate on the occasion of his (Fronto's) taking up the office of consul, part of which was devoted to honoring Faustina (*circa Faustinae meae honorem*). That he is referring to the Younger Faustina rather than to his deceased wife is made clear by his next remark: "By heaven, I would sooner live with her in Gyara than in the palace without her." This speech presumably would have been much like Pliny the Younger's *Panegyricus*, which Pliny also delivered in the Senate on the occasion of taking up his consulship, and in which he also mentioned (at some length) the virtues of Trajan's wife and sister. It is a shame that we do not know the exact way in which Fronto discussed Faustina in this speech, for it would certainly shed light on her public persona. A broad hint at the probable nature of the praise may be gained from the *Panegyricus*, where Plotina is lauded for her old-fashioned virtue, modesty and obedience ("for the glory of obedience is enough for a wife" *nam uxori sufficit obsequi gloria*).[5]

The next mentions of Faustina in the letters of Fronto are less cheering. The index (many letters are preserved only by their titles in the index) gives the opening line of a letter from Fronto to Marcus datable ca. 145–147, beginning *si animus Faustinae* "if Faustina's courage:"

2. See Chapter 1 for the nature of the text; the translations that follow are those of C. R. Haines in the Loeb edition.
3. Champlin 1974, 156.
4. *Ad Ant. Pium* 2; Loeb vol. I, pp. 126–128.
5. Pliny, *Pan.* 83.

some challenging event or circumstance is clearly being alluded to.[6] Four complete letters from this same time period report serious illness of both Faustina and her daughter, Annia. In three of them, two from Fronto and one from Marcus, Fronto writes that he has heard that Faustina is ill with fever, and Marcus replies that it is true but that she has lightened his mind "by being such an obedient patient" (*Ad M. Caes* v. 6, v. 10, and v. 11).[7] A letter of Marcus (*Ad. M. Caes* iv. 11) describes the illness of Annia Galeria Faustina (*parvola nostra Faustina*, "our dear little Faustina"); having recovered from diarrhea and fever, she is very emaciated and still suffers from a cough, but if the gods are willing, there is hope of improvement (*volentibus dis spem salutis nancisci videmur*).[8] A little later we learn that she is better: Marcus writes to Fronto (*Ad. M. Caes.* v. 24) "I am much relieved by the news of my little lady (*domnula mea*) telling me, the Gods be praised, that she is better."[9]

And there are also happier events reported. A celebration (*festa*, perhaps a birthday) is mentioned, which Fronto cannot attend due to a continuing illness of his feet, but he sends instructions for Marcus to kiss "our little ladies" (*matronas nostras*) also on their hands and feet (*Ad M. Caes.* v. 42 and 43).[10] Soon after, Marcus expresses concern for an impending birth (*Ad M. Caes.* v. 45: *eo accedit adpropinquatio partus Faustinae*).[11] Another letter records Fronto's excitement at seeing the newborn child: "To my Lord. I love you ten times as much - I have seen your daughter! At the same time it seemed I saw you and Faustina as infants: so much that is good in both your faces is blended in hers."[12] Unfortunately the dates of neither of these letters are known, and indeed their original order may have been the reverse, for this book of Fronto's letters (*Ad M. Caes.*) appears to have been arranged thematically, not chronologically.[13]

The next mention of children does not come until Marcus is emperor. A birthday greeting to Fronto from Marcus is apparently set shortly after the birth of Commodus and his twin brother Antoninus (*Ad Ant. Imp.* i. 1). Faustina is described as "recovering" (*reficit sanitatem*), presumably after the birth; Antoninus, "our little chick" (*pullus noster*) has a cough, and "the occupants of our little nest, each as far as he is old enough to do so, offer prayers for you" (*Quantum quisque in nidulo nostro iam sapit, tantum pro te precatur*).[14] The twins were born on August 31, 161.[15] In a couple of months Antoninus appears to have recovered, as he and his brother Commodus are described by Fronto (*Ad Ant. Imp.* i. 3) as having "quite a healthy color and strong lungs" (*sunt ... colore satis salubri clamore forti*).[16] This is the last mention of the children of Marcus and Faustina in the preserved letters of Fronto, who died in 166 or 167.[17]

6. Loeb vol. I, 190–191.
7. *Ad M. Caes* v.6, v.10 and v.11; Loeb vol. I, 192–195.
8. *Ad M. Caes* iv.11; Loeb vol. I, 202–203.
9. *Ad M. Caes.* v. 24, Loeb vol. I, 212–213.
10. *Ad M. Caes.* v. 42 and v. 43; Loeb I, 244–247.
11. *Ad M. Caes.* v. 45, Loeb I, 246–247.
12. *Ad M. Caes.* v. 52, Loeb I, 250–251, trans. Haines adapted.
13. For the organization of the correspondence, see Champlin 1974, 145.
14. *Ad Ant. Imp.* 1.1.
15. SHA *Commodus* 1.2: *natus est apud Lanuvium cum fratre Antonino gemino pridie kal. Sept. patre patruoque consulibus.*
16. *Ad Ant. Imp.* I, 3; Loeb II, 118–121.
17. On the date of death of Fronto, see Champlin 1974, 137–139.

Of particular note in these extracts from Fronto's letters is the fact that the chronology and context of the remarks, as best they can be reconstructed, appear to conform to the broad outline of commemoration of children on Faustina's coinage. Especially striking is the gap between the birth of Faustina's second (or third) child, ca. 150, and the birth of the twins Antoninus and Commodus in 161. This does not exactly correspond to the coinage, where births in 157 and 160 appear to be indicated (see Appendix 1), but there is nonetheless a gap during which we know that at least three children were born, but were not mentioned.

The letters also give us a very intimate glimpse into the family of Faustina, where we see normal human cares, concerns, and causes for joy. It is unfortunate, though perhaps not unexpected, that we have no information from Faustina herself. To run the risks of pregnancy so often, and to be ill more than once, must have weighed even more heavily on her than on Marcus. The dominance of the type Salus on her gold coinage in the early 160s brings the health of Faustina into a very public view. From a Roman male perspective, these risks appear to have been considered worth running to ensure the future of the empire. Pliny the Younger (*Pan.* 22) writes of women experiencing "the greatest pleasure" (*maxima voluptas*) when they saw Trajan because their *fecunditas* allowed them to produce citizens (*cives*) and soldiers (*milites*) for the *princeps*.[18] Obviously Pliny is a poor authority for the personal feelings of Roman women, but he is good evidence of how Roman men thought about Roman women, and his line of thinking has strong parallels with the very strong focus on motherhood that we see on Faustina's coinage.[19]

In the correspondence of Fronto, Faustina appears as an object of affection and concern to the men in her life, and especially to her husband Marcus. This evidence stands in striking contrast to how Faustina is often portrayed by historians who rely on the "evidence" of Cassius Dio and the *Historia Augusta* and fixate on the salacious and dramatic anecdotes they provide: that Faustina committed adultery with a gladiator, resulting in the birth of the deranged Commodus; that Faustina secretly convinced Avidius Cassius, governor of Syria, to stage his rebellion against her own husband; that she committed suicide in order to avoid punishment for this act; and that Lucius Verus "defiled" Faustina, causing her to plot to kill him with poison.[20] Levick is inclined to reject all stories of Faustina's supposed infidelity "as part of a single genre."[21] The contemporary evidence of coinage produced in Faustina's name, together with the correspondence of Fronto, supports this assessment. The later literary sources cannot be taken at face value; it is the coinage and the other rare contemporary accounts that give us a true glimpse of how Faustina was actually perceived by those who knew her, whether intimately, as members of her family or at a distance, as members of the public who saw her image in sculpture or on a coin.

18. On which see Boymel Kampen 1996, 21.
19. On Pliny and the ideal of the Roman wife, see Shelton 2013, 93–176 and Shelton 1990.
20. *SHA Marcus* 19 (gladiator); *SHA Marcus* 24, and Cassius Dio 72.22 (Avidius Cassius); Cassius Dio 72.29 (suicide); *SHA Verus* 10 (relationship with Verus).
21. Levick 2014, 82.

Appendix 1

Faustina's Children

The coinage, placed in its proper order by the die analysis, is a useful aid in establishing the probable sequence of births and deaths of the children of Faustina and Marcus Aurelius. Its key contribution is the arrangement of types between ca. 157 and 161 that depict a steadily increasing number of children. That these depictions do in fact reflect the actual number of children alive at the time they were produced is not certain, but there is some suggestion in the results of the die analysis that, at least some of the time, the correlation is valid. The evidence and arguments for the number, names and sequence of the children of Faustina and Marcus Aurelius are extensive. In order to keep the numismatic contribution in the forefront I do not repeat most of this material here, but rather direct the reader to the detailed reasoning of Ameling, or to Levick for an English summary.[1] Instead I have restricted this discussion to what is absolutely necessary to establish basic facts of the existence of a child and roughly the length of time he or she survived.

The coinage of ca. AD 157 provides a key point of reference (see Chapter 4). It suggests that, with the birth in that year, three children were now alive. The identification of the two children alive before this birth in AD 157 is straightforward. They must be:

Lucilla, who survived long enough to marry Lucius Verus when he was co-emperor with Marcus Aurelius. If she was born in 149, she would be about 8 years old.

Annia Faustina, who appears to have survived her father. She is named on a statue base at Eleusis: Φαυστεῖνα / Θεοῦ / Ἀντωνίνου / θυγάτηρ.[2] Since the only other daughter with

---

1. Ameling 1992; Levick 2014, 112–118.
2. *IEleusis* 509. A fully preserved marble base. This dedication was part of a group that also included Divus Antoninus (=Marcus Aurelius; *IEleusis* 504), Diva Faustina (*I. Eleusis* 506), (Vibia) Sabina, daughter of Divus Antoninus (*IEleusis* 508) and Lucilla, daughter of Divus Antoninus, with her name erased (*IEleusis* 505). Ameling (1992, 151, n. 19) notes that this is evidence that the group of statues was dedicated before the end of 181 (when Lucilla was murdered on the orders of Commodus).

the cognomen Faustina (Domitia Faustina) had died before Marcus became emperor (see immediately below), this must be Annia Faustina. Her date of birth is uncertain, but it was later than that of Lucilla (or she, rather than Lucilla, would have been betrothed to Verus).[3]

Three further children are known to have been born and died before Marcus became emperor. They are named as children of Marcus Caesar on funerary inscriptions from the Mausoleum of Hadrian. The inscriptions read:[4]

Domitia Faustina M. Aurelii Caesaris filia imp Anonini Augusi Pii pp. neptis (CIL 6.995 = *ILS* 385).

T. Aurelius Antoninus M. Aurelii Caesaris filius imp. Antonini Augusti Pii pp. nepos (CIL 6.993 = *ILS* 383).

T. Aelius Aurelius M. Aurelii Caesaris et Faustinae Aug. filius imp. Antonini Augusti Pii [pp.] nepos (CIL 6.994 = *ILS* 384).

A sixth child may also have been born in this period, the T. Aelius Antoninus named on a statue base from the Odeion of Herodes Atticus at Olympia, although it is possible he is equivalent to either number *CIL* 6.993 or 994, above.[5] If he existed as an independent entity, he was (according to the evidence of the coinage) deceased before 157.

Thus before the birth in AD 157 Faustina had borne at least five children, only two of whom (Lucilla and Annia Faustina) were still alive. Coins of Pius dated 156 show Pietas sheltering two children.[6] The third child, born in 157, Fadilla, survived at least till the end of Commodus's sole reign.[7]

The addition of a further child in the standing Fecunditas *aureus* type (die link Group 13, Fig. 4.4) ca. 159 or 160 brings the total number of children represented on coins to four. The child was presumably Cornificia, who lived long enough to be forced to commit suicide by Caracalla (Cass. Dio 78.16.6). The birth of the twins Commodus and Fulvus Antoninus in 161 is celebrated on coinage of Faustina, Marcus, and Pius; a total of six children are now shown on Faustina's coinage (Pair 13 for the twins on a throne with the legend *saeculi felicit(as)*, Group 14 for six children and a standing figure with the legend *tempor(um) felic(itas)*; both use the all-round legend format; Fig. 4.4). After this, children are no longer depicted on Faustina's *aurei*. One birth appears to be hinted at by the issue of types Laetitia and Venus Genetrix (Chain 7 in Fig. 4.9). The dominant theme of the reverse type Salus suggests an illness of Faustina herself. The *SHA* (*Comm.* 1.4) relates that Fulvus Antoninus, twin brother

3. Raepsaet-Charlier, *FOS* 61, has Annia Faustina as the first child born to Marcus and Faustina, based on the *Fasti Ostienses* for November 30, 147, which reads ...]*nnia Faustina filia nata est*. Raepsaet-Charlier would apparently reconstruct this as simply *Annia Faustina filia nata est*. But Vidman (tablet Pb, l. 14) more convincingly gives *ex A]nnia Faustina*, that is, "from Faustina the Younger." This is supported by Vidman (table Qa, l. 11), which records the birth of a son so: ...*ex An]nia Faustina filius n[atus*.

4. The inscriptions, no longer preserved, were recorded in the *codex Einsiedlensis*.

5. Bol 1984, 117–119. T. Ailios Antoneios, son of Marcus Aurelius Caesar, shares the pedestal with Annia Galeria Aurelia Faustina. Bol (1984, 37), presumably following Fittschen (1982, 23), interprets Aelius Antoninus as a child distinct from Aelius Aurelius and Aurelius Antoninus, whom she assigns to a twin birth of 149. Ameling (1992, 156), however, concludes that Aelius Antoninus of Olympia is "aller Wahrscheinlichkeit nach" the same person as one of the two boys commemorated in the Mausoleum of Hadrian inscriptions.

6. *BMCRE* Pius 857–858, *denarii*. Fittschen (1982, 28, n. 40) interprets this as evidence that only two children were alive in this year.

7. Herodian (1.13) casts her as denouncer of Cleander to Commodus (ca. 189) and calls her the oldest surviving sister of the emperor.

of Commodus, died at the age of four, so in 165. Three more children were born to Faustina after 161:

Annius Verus, who was made Caesar but died as a result of an operation on a tumour, according to the *SHA* (*Marc.* 21.3), just before Marcus set off for the German war. Since this occurred in 169, and the *SHA* gives the child's age as seven, a birth year of ca. 162–163 is implied.[8]

Hadrianus, named in an inscription from Ephesus: Ἀδριανὸν / υἱὸν Μ. Αὐρηλίου / Ἀντωνείνου / Καίσαρος Σεβαστοῦ.[9] He appears to have been a late son of Marcus and Faustina, born perhaps between Annius Verus and Vibia Sabina (see next); the resulting sequence of names (Hadrianus, Sabina) has a convincing ring.[10]

Vibia Sabina is known as a daughter of Marcus Aurelius from a number of inscriptions, and one from Numidia makes it clear that she survived the reign of Septimius Severus, by naming her *divi Severi soror*: *Vibiae Au/relliae di/vi M(arci) f(iliae) divi / Severi sor(orae) / Sabinae / patronae / municipii / decurio[num decreto].*[11] She was a sister of Severus after the latter had himself retroactively adopted by Marcus Aurelius, as part of his plans for justifying his claim to power.

This brings us to a total of twelve children: the six alive in 161, plus the three who died before the death of Antoninus Pius, plus the three who were born after 161. The total might be as high as thirteen, if the T. Aelius Antoninus from the Odeion of Herodes Atticus was in fact an independent entity, and not the same person as one of two sons known from the Mausoleum inscriptions.

---

8. *SHA Marc.* 21.3: *sub ipsis profectionis diebus in secessu Praenestino agens filium nomine Verum Caesarem exsecto sub aure tubere septennem amisit.* The *profectio* is refered to at *SHA Marc.* 20.6, *proficiscens ad bellum Germanicum*, set in the context of a shortened period of mourning for Lucius Verus (died 169); coins of Marcus with the type PROFECTIO AVG were struck in 169 (*BMCRE* Marcus 1349, 1350).

9. McCabe 1043.

10. This inscription was part of another family group, which included both Commodus (McCabe 1040; his name is erased) and Lucilla (McCabe 1042), who is not called Augusta; this suggests a date between 161 (birth of Commodus) and either 164 (when Lucilla married Verus) or ca. 166 (when her first child was born). Ameling (1992, 160), working from the idea that Lucilla received the title Augusta upon her marriage to Commodus (ca. AD 164), concludes that in this time-frame there is "kein Platz mehr für ein weiteres Kind." Thus he places the birth of Hadrianus before 159, interprets him as identical to one of the two sons named in the Mausoleum inscriptions, and requires us to understand this dedication to Hadrianus as a posthumous one. Fittschen (1982, 72–73) on the other hand argues in favor of Lucilla being awarded the title Augusta on the birth of her first child, following the model of Faustina, and supports it with reference to the coins.

11. *CIL* 8.5328 = *ILS* 388.

Appendix 2
Relative Proportions of Reverse Types in AV and AR

This appendix gives the relative proportions of the reverse types on the gold and silver coinage produced in Faustina's name. For the gold, the percentage of each type has been calculated based on the count in the *aureus* die study; for the silver, the percentage is based on the totals in the Reka Devnia hoard (RD).[1] For the sake of comparison between the two metals, the periodization has been left broad. For the gold it would be possible to subdivide these periods, but for the silver it would not, since no images of the Reka Devnia hoard coins are available in order to study their portraits.

1. Mouchmov 1934. The counts are taken from the portion of the hoard that is now in Sofia, numbering 68,783 coins. The 12,261 coins from the hoard now in Varna have been excluded, on the basis of the caution of C. Clay (in the 2003 reprint of Mouchmov) that the Varna list contains numerous errors and omissions.

AV under Pius

Reverse Inscription	Type	Number of Dies	Percentage
LAETITIAE PVBLICAE	Laetitia standing	9	7
IVNONI LVCINAE	Juno	4	3
VENERI GENETRICI	Venus, apple, child	7	6
"	Venus, apple, staff	4	3
VENVS	Venus, apple, rudder	26	21
IVNO	Juno seated, 2 children	5	4
CONCORDIA	Concordia standing	7	6
VENERI FELICI	bird	3	2
CONCORDIA	bird	28	22
VENVS	Venus, apple, staff	9	7
AVGVSTI PII FIL	Diana, bow and arrow	22	17
DIANA LVCIFERA	Diana, torch	1	1
FECVNDITATI AVGVSTAE	Fecunditas, 3 children	1	1

AR under Pius

Reverse Inscription	Type	Number in RD	Percentage
LAETITIAE PVBLICAE	Laetitia	26	4
PVDICITIA	Pudicitia (w or w/o altar)	105	15
CONCORDIA	Concordia (stg or std)	243	34
VENVS	Venus, apple, rudder	53	8
AVGVSTI PII FIL	Venus, victory, shield	122	17
"	Concordia	34	5
"	Spes	124	17

AV under Marcus

Reverse Inscription	Type	Number of Dies	Percentage
DIANA LVCIF	Diana, torch	5	6
IVNONI LVCINAE	Juno, 3 children	8	10
FECVNDITATI AVGVSTAE	Fecunditas, 3 children	7	9
FECVND AVGVSTAE	Fecunditas, 4 children	2	2
SAECVLI FELICIT	2 children on throne	2	2
TEMPOR FELEC	female, 6 children	2	2
SALVTI AVGVSTAE	Salus seated	35	41
LAETITIA	Laetitia standing	1	1
VENVS GENETRIX	Venus, Victory	1	1
CONCORDIA	Concordia seated	1	1
VENVS VICTRIX	Venus, Victory	2	2
HILARITAS	Hilaritas, palm	7	9

IVNO	Juno, staff	1	1
MATRI MAGNAE	Cybele	8	10
VENVS FELIX	Venus, Three Graces	2	2
MATRI CASTRORVM	female, standards	1	1

AR under Marcus

Reverse Inscription	Type	Number in RD	Percentage
DIANA LVCIF	Diana Lucifera	59	4
FECVND AVGVSTAE	Fecunditas, 4 children	97	7
TEMPOR FELIC	female, 4 children	8	1
SAECVLI FELICIT	throne, 2 children	180	13
FECVNDITAS	Fecunditas, 1 child	263	19
FORTVNAE MVLIEBRI	Fortuna	31	2
SALVS	Salus	114	8
HILARITAS	Hilaritas	186	14
IVNO	Juno (mainly seated)	35	3
CERES	Ceres (mainly seated)	114	8
IVNONI REGINAE	Juno (mainly standing)	196	15
LAETITIA	Laetitia, wreath, scepter	34	2
MATRI MAGNAE	Cybele	28	2
VENERI AVGVSTAE	Venus	12	1
VENERI VICTRICI	Venus	3	1

Bibliography

ABBREVIATIONS

BMCRE: H. Mattingly (et al.), *Coins of the Roman Empire in the British Museum*. London 1923–1962. (6 vols. Vol. IV covers the Antonines; individual coins are listed by emperor, then catalogue number.)

CIL: *Corpus Inscriptionum Latinarum*. Berlin 1863–.

IEleusis: K. Clinton, *Eleusis. The Inscriptions on Stone. Documents of the Sanctuary of the Two Goddesses and Public Documents of the Deme*. Athens 2005–2008.

IGR: R. Cagnat, *Inscriptiones Graecae ad res Romanas pertinentes*. Paris 1906–1927 (4 vols.).

ILS: H. Dessau (ed.), *Inscriptiones Latinae Selectae*. Berlin 1892–1916 (5 vols.).

LTUR: E. M. Steinby (ed.), *Lexicon Topographicum Urbis Romae*. Rome 1993–1999 (5 vols.).

Magister Gregorius: Magister Gregorius, *Narracio de mirabilibus urbis Romae*, R. B. C. Huygens (ed.). Leiden, 1970.

McCabe: D. F. McCabe, *Ephesos Inscriptions*. Princeton 1991.

OLD: P. G. W. Glare (ed.), *Oxford Latin Dictionary*. Oxford 1982.

Raepsaet-Charlier, *FOS*: M.–Th. Raepsaet-Charlier, *Prosopographie des femmes de l'ordre senatorial: Ier–IIer siècles*. Louvain 1987.

RE: A. Pauly, G. Wissowa, and W. Kroll (eds.), *Real-Encyclopädie der klassischen Altertumswisssenschaft*. Stuttgart 1893–1963.

RIC III: H. Mattingly and E. A. Sydenham, *The Roman Imperial Coinage III: From Antoninus Pius to Commodus*. London 1930.

TLL: *Thesaurus Linguae Latinae*. Leipzig 1900–.

Vidman: L. Vidman, *Fasti Ostienses*. Prague 1982.

BIBLIOGRAPHY

Alexandridis, A. 2004. *Die Frauen des römischen Kaiserhauses*. Mainz: Philipp von Zabern.

Alföldy, G. 1985. *The Social History of Rome*. London: Croom Helm.

Ameling, W. 1992. Die Kinder des Marc Aurel und die Bildnistypen der Faustina Minor. *Zeitschrift für Papyrologie und Epigraphik* 90: 147–166.

Barnes, T. D. 1978. *The Sources of the* Historia Augusta. Collection Latomus, 155. Brussels: Latomus.

Bartman, E. 2001. Hair and the Artifice of Roman Female Adornment. *American Journal of Archaeology* 105: 1–25.

———. 2012. Early Imperial Female Portraiture. In *A Companion to Women in the Ancient World*, edited by S. L. James and S. Dillon, 414–422. Malden, MA: Wiley-Blackwell.

Beckmann, M. 2007. Trajan's Gold Coinage, AD 112–117. *American Journal of Numismatics* 19: 77–129.

———. 2009. The Significance of Roman Imperial Coin Types. *Klio* 91: 144–161.

———. 2012. *DIVA FAUSTINA. Coinage and Cult in Rome and the Provinces*. New York: American Numismatic Society.

Bergmann, M. 1978. *Marc Aurel*. Frankfurt: Liebieghaus.

Bernoulli, J. J. 1891. *Römische Ikonographie* 2.2. Stuttgart: Union Deutsche Verlagsgesellschaft.

Birley, A. 1987. *Marcus Aurelius: A Biography*. Revised Edition. New Haven: Yale University Press.

Bol, R. 1984. *Das Statuenprogramm des Herodes-Atticus-Nymphäums*. Olympische Forschungen, 15. Berlin: Walter de Gruyter.

Boschung, D. 1993. *Die Bildnisse des Augustus. Das römische Herrscherbild* I.2. Berlin: Gebr. Mann.

Brendel, O. 1931. *Ikonographie des Kaisers Augustus*. Nürnberg: Buchdruckerei E. Kreller.

Champlin, E. 1974. The Chronology of Fronto. *Journal of Roman Studies* 64: 136–159.

Claes, L. 2014. A Note on the Coin Type Selection by the *a rationibus*. *Latomus* 73: 163–173.

Duff, J. W. 1936. Social Life in Rome and Italy. In *The Cambridge Ancient History* (1st ed.), vol. XI, edited by J. B. Bury et al., 753–774. Cambridge: Cambridge University Press.

Duncan-Jones, R. 1994. *Money and Government in the Roman Empire*. Cambridge: Cambridge University Press.

Egger, A. E., ed. 1838. *M. Verrii Flacci, Fragmenta; Sexti Pompei Festi, Fragmentum*. Paris: Bourgeois-Maze.

Elkins, N. T. 2017. *The Image of Political Power in the Reign of Nerva, AD 96–98*. Oxford: Oxford University Press.

Esty, W. E. 1990. The Theory of Linkage. *Numismatic Chronicle* 150: 205–221.

———. 2006. How to estimate the original number of dies and the coverage of a sample. *Numismatic Chronicle* 166: 359–364.

_____. 2011. The geometric model for estimating the number of dies. In *Quantifying Monetary Supplies in Greco-Roman Times*, edited by F. de Callataÿ, 43–58. Bari: Edipuglia.

Fejfer, J. 1998. The Roman Emperor Portrait. Some Problems in Methodology. *Ostraka* 7: 45–56.

_____. 2008. *Roman Portraits in Context.* Berlin: Walter de Gruyter.

Fittschen, K. 1971. Zum Angeblichen Bildnis des Lucius Verus in Thermen-Museum. *Jahrbuch des Deutschen Archäologischen Instituts* 86: 214–252.

_____. 1982. *Die Bildnistypen der Faustina minor und die Fecunditas Augustae.* Göttingen: Vandenhoeck & Ruprecht.

_____. 1999. *Prinzenbildnisse antoninischer Zeit.* Mainz: Philipp von Zabern.

_____. 2010. The portraits of Roman emperors and their families. Controversial positions and unsolved problems. In *The emperor and Rome. Space, representation and ritual*, edited by B. C. Ewald and C. F. Noreña, 221–246. Cambridge: Cambridge University Press.

Fittschen, K. and P. Zanker. 1983. *Katalog der romischen Porträts in den Capitolinischen Museen und den anderen kommunalen Sammlungen der Stadt Rom. III. Kaiserinnen- und Prinzessinnenbildnisse, Frauenporträts.* Mainz: Philipp von Zabern.

_____. 2014. *Katalog der romischen Porträts in den Capitolinischen Museen und den anderen kommunalen Sammlungen der Stadt Rom. IV. Kinderbildnisse, Nachträge zu den Bänden I–III, neuzeitliche oder neuzeitlich verfälschte Bildnisse, Bildnisse an reliefdenkmälern.* Berlin: Walter de Gruyter.

Fündling, J. 2016. Review of *Faustina I and II. Imperial Women of the Golden Age* by Barbara M. Levick, *H-Soz-Kult*, 21.03.2016. www.hsozkult.de/publicationreview/id/reb-21373.

Gibbon, E. 1776. *The Decline and Fall of the Roman Empire.* Vol. I. D. Womersley ed. (1994), London: Penguin.

Gilles, K.-J. 2013. *Der römische Goldmünzschatz aus der Feldstraße in Trier.* Trier: Rheinisches Landesmuseum.

Gnecchi, F. 1912. *I Medaglioni Romani.* Milan: Ulrico Hoepli.

Grierson, P., 1975. *Numismatics.* London: Oxford University Press.

Hahn, U. 1994. *Die Frauen des römischen Kaiserhauses und ihre Ehrungen im griechischen Osten anhand epigraphischer und numismatischer Zeugnisse von Livia bis Sabina.* Saarbrücken: Saarbrücker Druckerei und Verlag.

Hallett, C. H. 2007. Review of *Roman Imperial Statue Bases: From Augustus to Commodus*, by J. M. Højte. *Journal of Roman Studies* 97: 342–343.

Hamilton, C. D. 1969. The Tresviri Monetales and the Republican Cursus Honorum. *Transactions and Proceedings of the American Philological Association* 100: 181–199.

Højte, J. M. 2005. *Roman Imperial Statue Bases From Augustus to Commodus.* Aarhus: Aarhus University Press.

Honoré, T. 1987. Scriptor Historiae Augustae. *Journal of Roman Studies* 77: 156–176.

Howgego, C. J. 1995. *Ancient History from Coins.* London: Routledge.

Kampen, N. B. 1996. Gender Theory in Roman Art. In *I Claudia. Women in Ancient Rome*, edited by D. E. E. Kleiner and S. B. Mathenson, 14–25. New Haven: Yale University Press.

Kienast, D. 1990. *Römische Kaisertabelle: Grundzüge einer römischen Kaiserchronologie.* Darmstadt: Wissenschaftliche Buchgesellschaft.

Kropp, A. 2008. Statue Bases. Review of *Roman Imperial Statue Bases. From Augustus to Commodus*, by J. M. Højte. *Classical Review* 58.1: 283–285.

Levick, B. M. 1982. Propaganda and the Imperial Coinage. *Antichthon* 16: 104–116.

_____. 1999. Messages on the Roman Coinage: Types and Inscriptions. In *Roman Coins and Public Life Under the Empire: E. Togo Salmon Papers II*, edited by G. Paul and M. Ierardi, 41–60. Ann Arbor: University of Michigan Press.

_____. 2014. *Faustina I and II. Imperial Women of the Golden Age*. Oxford: Oxford University Press.

Metcalf, W. E. 1996. Roman Dies in Modern Studies. In *Italiam fato profugi Hesperinaque venerunt litora. Numismatic Studies Dedicated to Vladimir and Elvira Eliza Clain-Stefanelli*, 253–258. Louvain-la-Neuve: Département d'Archéologie et d'Histoire de l'Art, Séminaire de Numismatique Marcel Hoc.

Meyers, R. 2016. *Filiae Augustorum*: The Ties That Bind in the Antonine Age. *Classical World* 109.4: 487–505.

Mikocki, T. 1995. *Sub Specie Deae. Les Impératrices et Princesses Romaines Assimilées à des Déesses*. Rome: Bretschneider.

Millar, F. 1964. *A Study of Cassius Dio*. Oxford: Clarendon Press.

Mittag, P. F. 2012. *Römische Medaillons 1. Caesar bis Hadrian*. 2nd ed. Stuttgart: Franz Steiner.

_____. 2019. *Römische Medaillons II. Antoninus Pius*. Stuttgart: Franz Steiner.

Mongez, A. 1826. *Iconographie Romaine* III. Paris: Jules Didot.

Mouchmov, N. A. 1934. *Le Trésor numismatique de Réka Devnia (Marcianopolis)*. Sofia: Imprimerie de l'état.

Olson, K. 2008. *Dress and the Roman Woman: Self-Presentation and Society*. New York: Routledge.

Peachin, M. 1986. The *Procurator Monetae*. *Numismatic Chronicle* 146: 94–106.

Pfanner, M. 1989. Über das Herstellen von Porträts. *Jahrbuch des Deutschen Archäologischen Instituts* 104: 157–257.

Riccardi, L. A. 2007. Review of Fittschen 1999. *American Journal of Archaeology* 111.1: online publication: https://www.ajaonline.org/book-review/485.

Ridgway, B. S. 1986. The State of Research on Ancient Art. *The Art Bulletin* 68: 7–23.

Shelton, J.-A. 1990. Pliny the Younger, and the Ideal Wife. *Classica et Medievalia* 41: 163–186.

_____. 2013. *The Women of Pliny's Letters*. New York: Routledge.

Smith, R. R. R. 1983. Review of *Die Bildnistypen der Faustina Minor und die Fecunditas Augustae*, by K. Fittschen. *Journal of Roman Studies* 73: 228–229.

Speidel, M. A. 2012. *Faustina—mater castrorum*. Ein Beitrag zur Religionsgeschichte. *Tyche* 27: 127–152.

Stavridis, A. 1987. Ein Porträt der Faustina Minor im Akropolismuseum. *Römische Mitteilungen* 94: 107–108.

Strack, P. L. 1933. *Untersuchungen zur römischen Reichsprägung des zweiten Jahrhunderts*. Teil II. *Die Reichsprägung zur Zeit des Hadrian*. Stuttgart: Kohlhammer.

_____. 1937. *Untersuchungen zur römischen Reichsprägung des zweiten Jahrhunderts*. Teil III. *Die Reichsprägung zur Zeit des Antoninus Pius*. Stuttgart: Kohlhammer.

Stephens, J. 2008. Ancient Roman hairdressing: on (hair)pins and needles. *Journal of Roman Archaeology* 21: 110–132.

Sutherland, C. H. V. 1970. *The Cistophori of Augustus*. London: Royal Numismatic Society.

———. 1986. Compliment or Complement? Dr Levick on Imperial Coin Types. *The Numismatic Chronicle* 146: 85–93.

Swindler, M. H. 1923. Venus Pompeiana and the New Pompeian Frescoes. *American Journal of Archaeology* 27: 302–313.

Thilo, G., and H. Hagen, eds. 1881–1902. *Servii Grammatici qvi fervntvr in Vergilii carmina commentarii*. Leipzig: B. G. Teubner.

Trillmich, W. 1971. Zur Formgeschichte von Bildnis-Typen. *Jahrbuch des Deutschen Archäologischen Instituts* 86: 179–213.

Trunk, M. 1999. Zum 1. Bilnistypus der Faustina Minor. *Madrider Mitteilungen* 40: 218–227.

Von den Hoff, R. 2011. Kaiserbilnisse als Kaisergeschichte(n). Prolegomena zu einem medialen Konzept römischer Kaiserporträts. In *Zwischen Strukturgeschichte und Biographie. Probleme und Perspektiven einer neuen römischen Kaisergeschichte*, edited by A. Winterling, 15–44. Munich: De Gruyter Oldenbourg.

Walker, D. R. 1988. The Roman Coins. In *The Temple of Sulis Minerva at Bath. Volume 2. The Finds from the Sacred Spring*, edited by B. Cunliffe, 281–358. Oxford: Oxford University Committee for Archaeology.

Wallace-Hadrill, A. 1986. Image and Authority in the Coinage of Augustus. *Journal of Roman Studies* 76: 66–87.

———. 1996. The Imperial Court. In *The Cambridge Ancient History*, vol. X, edited by A. K. Bowman et al., 283–308. Cambridge: Cambridge University Press.

Wegner, M. 1939. *Die Herrscherbildnisse in antoninischer Zeit*. Berlin: Gebr. Mann.

Woytek, B. 2010. *Die Reichsprägung des Kaisers Traianus (98–117)*. Vienna: Verlag der Österreichischen Akademie der Wissenschaften.

———. 2012. System and Product in Roman Mints from the Late Republic to the High Principate: Some Current Problems. *Revue Belge de Numismatique et de sigillographie* 158: 85–122.

Zanker, P. 1973. *Studien zu den Augustus-Porträts I. Der Actium Typus*. Göttingen: Vanderhoeck & Ruprecht.

Die Catalogue, Part 1
Aurei of Faustina II under Antoninus Pius

The catalogue has two primary functions: first, when used together with the image files, to allow the reader to identify the dies of any new coin as simply as possible; and second, to allow any of the die identifications made herein to be checked by the reader. That is to say, the catalogue is mainly a tool for making and confirming die identifications; it is not intended to be used to understand or interpret the pattern of die-links that it documents. For this purpose, the reader should consult the graphic die-link charts, on which the dies, their links, and the number of specimens are all represented.

The catalogue developed as the die-study progressed, with the result that new coins and dies were added in the order that they were discovered. It has not been rearranged (the danger of introducing error through such a process is too great), and the order of listing in the catalogue should *not* be considered to represent chronological order. For this purpose, again, the reader must consult the graphic die-link charts. Alphabetical listing by reverse type was chosen to make die-identification as quick as possible, and the catalogue has been left in this format in order to easily identify the dies of newly found coins. Obverse dies are always labeled with lower-case letters, reverse dies with capitals. This has the benefit of making reverse types, which in general are more important for this coinage, stand out in the text.

Note on organization: The catalogue is organized in a hierarchical manner: first by emperor under which the coins were produced (Pius then Marcus), then (under Pius alone) by obverse inscription following the classification of Mattingly in *BMCRE* IV. Thus for the catalogue of coins produced **under Antoninus Pius, the entries under each individual reverse type often do not represent all the dies of that type,** if the type is used with obverse dies bearing different inscriptions. Also note that two obverse dies are shared between the last issues bearing

Faustina's filiation and issues without filiation. Finally, some dies have been removed during the course of the analysis. See notes below. The catalogue is presented as follows:

JL		IVNONI LVCINAE Juno standing l., holding patera in right hand, staff in left.
JL1	fa3	a. NAC K, 30 March 2000, 1853 = Christie's, 15 May 1990, 392.
	fa9	a. Tkalec and Astarte, 28 February 2007, 48. b. ANS 1958.223.1. c. Vienna 36790. d. Trier 2451.

In this entry, JL is the abbreviation for the reverse type Juno Lucina. A brief description of the type is given (normally after Mattingly in *BMCRE* IV). The dies are then listed. Reverse die JL1 is linked to two obverse dies, fa3 and fa9. The first combination (JL1/fa3) is represented by only one coin, which was sold in two auctions, once in 1990 and again in 2000 (auction files have been rigorously checked for duplication). Auction references are given in the format "Auction Company Name (and sale number), date, lot number." The second combination (JL1/fa9) is represented by four coins: one sold at auction in 2007, one in the collection of the ANS, one in the Münzkabinett of the Kunsthistorisches Museum in Vienna, and one found in the great Trier hoard. These abbreviated names are expanded in the list below.

A few coins in the catalogue sold at older auctions and preserved in the auction file catalogue of the British Museum do not have full information as to what auction they were sold in. This is because the key to the card file was destroyed, and it has only been possible to partially reconstruct it. So for a few entries one will see something like: " BM Card File, key #288 (no entry), 57." This means that the image of this coin is preserved in the British Museum card file, where it is marked with a handwritten number (228) that directs the user to the entry in the key that gives the name and date of the auction.

But "(no entry)" indicates this part of the key has been lost, so all we have is the handwritten reference and the lot number (57). These coins have, as with all auction coins, been double-checked for duplication where relevant.

ABBREVIATIONS AND COLLECTIONS

ANS	American Numismatic Society, New York.
Arquennes	Arquennes, Belgium. All recorded in the archive in Brussels, most sold at Spink, many but not all in catalogues 60 (7 October 1987), 65 (5 October 1988), and later auctions.
Augsburg	L. Weber, Ein Schatzfund römischer Aurei in Augsburg, *Jahrbuch des Römisch-Germanischen Zentralmuseums* 28 (1981): 133–171.
Berlin	Münzkabinett der Staatlichen Museen zu Berlin.

BMCRE   *Coins of the Roman Empire in the British Museum*, vol. IV. London 1940.

Madrid   Collection of the Archaeological Museum, Madrid. C. Alfaro Asins, *Catálogo de las monedas antiguas de oro del Museo Arqueológico Nacional*. Madrid 1993. Some of the coins were destroyed during the Spanish Civil War, and they are only known from rubbings made of them before their destruction; this is noted with the word "rubbing" in the relevant entries.

Paris   Département des Monnaies, Médailles et Antiques de la Bibliothèque nationale de France, Paris.

Sartiges   Collection of the Vicomte de Sartiges. *Collection du Vicomte de Sartiges: séries Grecque et Romaine en 1910 ainsi que les acquisitions depuis cette date*. Paris n.d.

Trier   Trier Feldstrasse Hoard, discovered 1993; coins currently in Landesmuseum, Trier.

            Complete report: K.-J. Gilles, *Der römische Goldmünzenschatz aus der Feldstrasse in Trier*. Trier 2013.

Via Po   Hoard found by the Via Po in Rome. S. L. Cesano, "Ripostiglio di *aurei* imperiali rinvenuto a Roma," *Bullettino della Commissione archeologica Comunale di Roma* 57 (1929) 1–119.

Vienna   Kunsthistoriches Museum Wien, Münzkabinett.

Notes on Specific Die Identities

ff3 under Antoninus Pius = fm15 under Marcus Aurelius ff5 under Antoninus Pius = fm6 under Marcus Aurelius CB20 removed (=CB3)
VA20 and fa27 (M&M, 17–19 June 1954, 709) removed (= denarius)

Catalogue of *Aurei* Issued Under Antoninus Pius

Obverse Legends

fa   FAVSTINAE AVG PII AVG FIL
[fb   FAVSTINA AVG PII AVG F - no aurei known with this legend]
fc   FAVSTINA AVG ANTONINI AVG PII FIL
fd   FAVSTINA AVG PII AVG FIL
fe   FAVSTINA AVGVSTA AVG PII F/FIL
ff   FAVSTINA AVGVSTA (reverse: AVGVSTI PII FIL or descriptive legend)

Summary of Reverse Types and Labels:

AD   AVGVSTI PII FIL Diana holding bow in l., arrow in r. hand.
C   CONCORDIA Female figure holding cornucopia.
CB   CONCORDIA Bird standing r.

JL   IVNONI LVCINAE Juno standing l., holding patera in right hand, staff in left.
JS   IVNO Juno seated l., child on knee, second child on ground.
LP   LAETITIAE PVBLICAE Female figure standing l., holding staff in left hand, wreath in r.
VA   VENVS Venus standing l., holding apple in right hand, left hand resting on upturned rudder.
VB   VENVS Venus standing l., holding apple in right hand, staff in left.
VF   VENERI FELICI Bird standing r.
VG   VENERI GENETRICI Venus standing l., holding apple in r., swaddled child in l.
VS   VENERI GENETRICI Venus standing l., holding apple in r., staff in l.

Group I (fa)   FAVSTINAE AVG PII AVG FIL

C   CONCORDIA Female holding cornucopia.

C3	fa7	a. *BMCRE* 1041.
		b. Trier 2448.
C5	fa7	a. Vinchon, 18 May 1994, 64.
		b. ANS 1956.184.56.
		c. Arquennes 719.

CB   CONCORDIA Bird (dove) standing r.

| CB22 | fa25 | a. Münzhandlung Basel, 22 March 1937, 798 = Hess, 24 May 1935, 1741. |
| CB27 | fa25 | a. Paris 962. |

JL   IVNONI LVCINAE Juno standing l., holding patera in right hand, staff in left.

JL1	fa3	a. NAC K, 30 March 2000, 1853 = Christie's, 15 May 1990, 392.
	fa9	a. Tkalec and Astarte, 28 February 2007, 48.
		b. ANS 1958.223.1.
		c. Vienna 36790.
		d. Trier 2451.
JL2	fa3	a. NAC 34, 24 November 2006, 169 = Glendining, 16–21 November 1950, 548.
		b. *BMCRE* 1045.
		c. Hess, 9 May 1951, 180.
		d. Paris 970.
JL3	fa9	a. Ars Classica, 12 June 1922, 966 = Feuardent, 2 April 1914, 402 (probably = Schulman, June 1966, 1902).

JL4   fa3   a. Ars Classica, 3 July 1933, 1870.

                    b. BM Card File, key #288 (no entry), 57.

JS   IVNO Juno seated l., child on knee, second child on ground.

JS1   fa7   a. CNG Triton XI, 8 January 2008, 944 = CNG Triton VIII, 11 January 2005, 1147.

                    b. Arquennes 720.

                    c. Paris, Edmond Rothschild 400.

                    d. Münzen und Medaillen, June 1959, 226.

                    e. Stack's Bowers and Ponterio, Sale 174, 11 January 2013, 5451.

        fa19   a. *BMCRE* 1044.

JS2   fa7   a. Leu 91, 10 May 2004, 571.

                    b. *BMCRE* 1043.

        fa19   a. Madrid (rubbing 265).

JS3   fa16   a. NAC 46, 2 April 2008, 1091.

JS4   fa19   a. Paris 969.

JS5   fa7   a. NFA, March 1976, 430.

LP   LAETITIAE PVBLICAE Female figure standing l., holding staff in left hand, garland in right.

LP1   fa1   a. Hess 257, 12 November 1986, 347.

                    b. Spink 5003, 31 March 2005, 160 = Waldeck Basel, March 1935, 558.

                    c. ANS 1001.1.22245.

                    d. ANS 1958.223.19.

                    e. Paris 973.

        fa15   a. *BMCRE* 1047

        fa28   a. CNG 36, 5–6 December 1995, 2410 = Lanz, November 1988, 555 = Christie's, 8 October 1985, 115.

                    b. Rollin & Feuardent, 20–28 April 1896, 411.

LP2   fa6   a. Tkalec, 22 April 2007, 236.

LP3   fa15   a. Baldwins etc. New York Sale XIV, 10 January 2007, 312.

                    b. Hess Divo 314, 4 May 2009, 1569 = NAC 45, 2 April 2008, 130.

                    c. NAC 49, 21 October 2008, 282.

                    d. Münzen und Medaillen 181, July 1958, 65.

                    e. Berlin 18203679.

LP4	fa6	a. Gemini Auction II, 11 January 2006, 478.
		b. Christie's, 8 October 1985, 58.
		c. Leu, May 1974, 184.
LP5	fa9	a. NAC 41, 20 November 2007, 103 = CNG Triton IV, 5 December 2000, 582.
LP6	fa3	a. ANS 1958.223.2.
	fa9	a. *BMCRE* 1046.
		b. ANS 1958.223.17.
		c. Hess-Leu, May 1970, 547.
LP7	fa15	a. ANS 1958.223.3.
		b. Hess, May 1982, 270.
LP8	fa6	a. Paris 103.
LP9	fa9	a. Madrid 406.
		b. Madrid (rubbing 267).

VA   VENVS Venus standing l., holding apple in right hand, left hand resting on upturned rudder.

VA1	fa2	a. NAC, 27 February 1991, 379.
		b. Leu 45, May 1988, 343.
VA2	fa4	a. NFA 27, 4–5 December 1991, 136.
		b. Vinchon, 24–26 April 1996, 73.
		c. NAC 31, 26 October 2005, 57.
		d. CNG 54, 14 June 2000, 1623.
	fa11	a. Künker 100, 21 June 2005, 63.
		b. Florange and Ciani, 4–5 May 1925, 280.
		c. Schulman, 5 March 1923, 1665.
	fa23	a. Vienna 35456.
	fa29	a. Münzen und Medaillen, December 1968, 329 = ANS 1958.223.18 (sold).
VA3	fa5	a. Vinchon 7, 22–23 May 1995, 340 = Arquennes 722.
VA4	fa7	a. Baldwin's etc. New York Sale XXIII, 6 January 2010, 179 = Hess-Leu, 14 April 1945, 319.
VA5	fa8	a. CNG, 22 February 2012, 371 = CNG Mail Bid 57, 4 April 2001, 1290 = Hess-Leu, 14 April 1945, 320 = Ars Classica, 16 June 1922, 75.
		b. Trier 2463.
	fa17	a. NAC 59, 4 April 2011, 1024 = NAC 25, 25 June 2003, 484.

        b. *BMCRE* 1065.

        c. Santamaria, 24 January 1938, 623.

        d. Arquennes 723.

        e. Madrid (rubbing 269).

VA6   fa10   a. CNG Mail Bid 82, 16 September 2009, 1023.

VA7   fa5   a. Heidelberger 48, 15 November 2007, 237 = Künker 124, 16 March 2007, 7638.

        b. Ars Classica, 12 June 1922, 981.

     fa14   a. *BMCRE* 1063.

        b. Rollin & Feuardent, 20–28 April 1896, 417.

     fa18   a. NAC 33, 6 April 2006, 505.

        b. Bourgey, 6–8 December 1978, 150 = Ars Classica, 3 July 1933, 1887.

        c. ANS 1958.223.15.

        d. Paris 983.

     fa21   a. Hess, 5 April 1955, 110 = Hamburger, 25 October 1932, 917.

VA8   fa11   a. Hess Divo 309, 28 April 2008, 167 = Bourgey, 15 December 1924, 29 = Schulman, 5 March 1923, 1664 = Hirsch, 13 November 1907, 612 = BM Card File, (no entry), 198.

        b. Egger, 15 January 1912, 1034 = BM Card File, key #32 (no entry), 1792.

        c. Trier 2462.

     fa12   a. Künker 112, 20 June 2006, 1014 = Künker 104, 27 September 2005, 535.

     fa14   a. Jesus Vico 120, 4 June 2009, 315 = NAC 51, 5 March 2009, 1032 = NAC R, 17 May 2007, 1549 = Glendining, 7–8 March 1957, 400.

        b. Via Po 377.

VA9   fa1   a. Heritage ANA Sale 3033, 8 August 2014, 23085.

     fa13   a. Leu 86, 5 May 2003, 865.

VA10   fa14   a. Leu 87, 6 May 2003, 34 = Leu, April 1972, 409.

VA11   fa4   a. Ars Classica, 18–20 June 1925, 633 = Rollin & Feuardent, 20–28 April 1896, 416.

     fa11   a. M&M Basel 95, 4 October 2004, 146.

        b. NAC 41, 20 November 2007, 102 = CNG Triton III, 30 November 1999, 1097.

        c. NAC 49, 21 October 2008, 281

        d. Madrid 409.

        e. Hess Leu, May 1965, 435.

VA12	fa13	a. UBS 78, 9 September 2008, 1690.
		b. Ars Classica, 3 October 1934, 852 = Ars Classica, 3 July 1933, 1889.
		c. Ars Classica, 10 October 1938, 269 = Hirsch, 23 May 1910, 754.
		d. Canessa, 28 June 1923, 384.
		e. Sartiges 210.
		f. Hess Nachf, 25 March 1929, 851 = Hirsch, May 1914, 1182 = BM Card File, key #124 (no entry), 160.
		g. Gorny 42, October 1988, 677.
		h. Sotheby's, 13 June 1911, 549.
		i. Arquennes 721.
		j. Paris, Armand Valton 1061.
VA13	fa22	a. Bourgey, 10 December 1923, 232.
VA14	fa10	a. Ball, 9 February 1932, 1692.
VA15	fa14	a. Berlin 18204219.
	fa21	a. Feuardent, 2 April 1914, 405.
	fa23	a. ANS 1966.62.20 = Canessa, 28 June 1923, 383 = Hirsch, 23 May 1910, 753.
VA16	fa24	a. Glendining, 20–21 November 1969, 116.
VA17	fa21	a. Hess, 8 May 1951, 183.
VA18	fa17	a. ANS 1001.1.22246.
	fa19	a. Glendining, 20 February 1951, 1803.
VA19	fa26	a. Hess-Lucerne, 18 December 1933, 622.
VA21	fa20	a. Christie's, 8 October 1985, 117.
VA22	fa4	a. Christie's, 6 Octover 1987, 441.
VA23	fa19	a. Paris 151.
		b. Trier 2461.
VA24	fa13	a. Vienna 12505.
VA25	fa21	a. J. Schulman, June 1966, 1904.
		b. CNG 96, 14 May 2014, 811.
VA26	fa2	a. Roma Numismatics 4, 30 September 2012, 564.

VG   VENERI GENETRICI Venus standing l., holding apple in r., swaddled child in l.

VG1	fa3	a. NFA 11, 8 December 1982, 449.
		b. NFA 14, 29 November 1984, 439 = Hess-Lucerne, 18 December 1933, 621 = Egger, 15 January 1912, 1031.

VG2   fa9   a. CNG Triton V, 15 January 2002, 1997.

a. Trier 2454.

VG3   fa5   a. Bourgey, 15 December 1924, 27.

fa6   a. *BMCRE* 1058.

VG4   fa1   a. Berk 34, 25 October 1984, 11L.

b. *BMCRE* 1060.

c. Madrid (rubbing 270).

VG5   fa9   a. *BMCRE* 1059.

VG6   fa6   a. Christie's, 22 April 1986, 472.

fa9   a. Santamaria, 23 October 1951, 66.

b. Christie's, 7 October 1986, 243.

VG7   fa6   a. ANS 1965.66.32.

VS   VENERI GENETRICI Venus standing l., holding apple in r., staff in l.

VS1   fa14   a. LHS 97, 10 May 2006, 31.

b. *BMCRE* 1057.

c. Rollin & Feuardent, 20–28 April 1896, 415.

d. Paris, Edmond Rothschild 402.

a. Trier 2453.

VS2   fa2   a. NAC 41, 20 November 2007, 101.

b. NAC 52, 7 October 2009, 467 = NAC 38, 21 March 2007, 77 = Leu, May 1973, 388.

c. NAC 31, 26 October 2005, 56.

d. CNG 16, 16 August 1991, 494.

e. Leu, April 1990, 319.

f. Hess-Leu, April 1971, 380.

fa18   a. Ars Classica, 3 July 1933, 1882 = Leu, May 1979, 276.

b. Ars Classica, 3 July 1933, 1883.

c. Münzhandlung Basel 6, 18 March 1936, 1780 = Ars Classica, 3 July 1933, 1884.

VS3   fa18   a. Canessa, 28 June 1923, 283 = Hirsch, 23 May 1910, 752.

b. Madrid 407.

VS4   fa18   a. Vienna 36792.

Group II (fc) FAVSTINA AVG ANTONINI AVG PII FIL

C   CONCORDIA Female figure holding Cornucopia.

C1   fc1   a. Künker 124, 16 March 2007, 7637.

          fc5   a. Christie's, 8 October 1985, 114.

C4   fc5   a. Rollin & Feuardent, 20–28 April 1896, 403.

CB   CONCORDIA Bird standing r.

CB16   fc3   a. Münzhandlung Basel 6, 18 March 1936, 1778 = Ars Classica, 3 October 1934, 1487.

                     b. Vienna 12432.

CB18   fc2   a. Hess-Leu, 14 April 1945, 314 = Ars Classica, 3 October 1934, 843.

CB26   fc2   a. ANS 1954.256.24.

VF   VENERI FELICI Bird standing r.

VF1   fc2   a. M&M Basel 93, 16 December 2003, 184.

                     b. M&M, 3–4 December 1948, 611.

VF2   fc2   a. *BMCRE* 1082.

                     b. *BMCRE* 1083.

                     c. Schulman, 27 February 1939, 61 = Drouot, 19–21 May, 1921, 1216.

                     d. Coin Galleries, 20 August 1986, 13 = Coin Galleries, 10 April 1985, 14.

                     e. ANS 1965.66.33.

                     f. Vienna 12503.

                     g. Trier 2452.

          fc6   a. Vinchon, 20 November 1992, 120.

VF3   fc2   a. Ars Classica, 25 June 1924, 1064.

          fc4   a. Christie's, 9 October 1984, 74.

Group IV (fd) FAVSTINA AVG PII AVG FIL

C   **CONCORDIA Female figure holding cornucopia.**

C2	fd12	a. Peus 369, 31 October 2001, 579 = Christie's, 8 October 1985, 113.
	fd15	a. *BMCRE* 1084.
		b. ANS 1955.191.15.
C6	fd24	a. Vienna 12435.
C7	fd12	a. Münzen und Medaillen, October 1988, 243.

CB   **CONCORDIA Bird standing r.**

CB1   fd1[1]   a. CNG Triton IX, 10 January 2006, 1494 = M&M Basel 95, 4 October 2004, 147 = NAC, 25 February 1992, 497.

b. NAC 51, 5 March 2009, 312 = Arquennes 727.

fd16   a. Ars Classica, 3 July 1933, 1862

CB2   fd1   a. Nomisma 47, 13 April 2013, 187 = NAC, 27 February 1991, 380 = NFA 14, 29 November 1984, 438.

b.[2] NAC, 3 April 1995, 851.

c. Baldwins 43, 11 October 2005, 2154.

d. Lanz 102, 28 May 2001, 627 = CNG 26, 11 June 1993, 495.

e. Bourgey, 27 March 1912, 303.

f. Hirsch, 17 November 1904, 190.

g. ANS 1958.223.5.

fd3   a. NAC 24, 5 December 2002, 110 = CNG Triton IV, 5 December 2000, 583.

b. Bourgey, 21–22 January 1992, 145.

fd6   a. Hess Divo 305, 25 October 2006, 35.

b. UBS 55, 16 September 2002, 1958 = Künker 67, 9 October 2001, 786.

c. Lanz 141, 26 May 2008, 459 = Cahn 75, 30 May 1933, 1209 = BM Card File, key #314 (no entry), 422.

d. Kress, 21 June 1954, 568.

1. Obverse shows die damage that does not appear on **CB2/fd1.a.**
2. The obverse die in this pairing (**CB2/fd1.b**) shows more wear than when used in the pair **CB1/fd1.a**, which in turn appears to show more wear/damage than **CB2/fd1.a**.

	fd22	a. Astarte 1, 11 May 1998, 263 = CNG 40, 4 December 1996, 1537 = NFA/Leu, 16 May 1984 (Garrett Coll. I), 813.
CB6	fd6	a. Hess Divo 314, 4 May 2009, 1568.
	fd13	a. UBS 78, 9 September 2008, 1689 = Santamaria, 24 January 1938, 615.
		b. Münzhandlung Basel 6, 18 March 1936, 1779 = Ars Classica, 3 July 1933, 1864.
		c. Ars Classica, 3 July 1933, 1865.
		d. Hess, 24 May 1935, 1736.
CB7	fd7	a. Künker 155, 24 June 2009, 3023 = Lanz 145, 5 January 2009, 119 = Auctiones, September 1985, 669.
		b. Künker 97, 7 March 2005, 1470.
		c. Ars Classica, 3 July 1933, 1861.
		d. Lanz, May 1984, 562.
		e. Münzen und Medaillen 64, January 1984, 259.
		f. Hess-Leu, March 1959, 356.
	fd14	a. ANS 2017.34.1 = UBS 78, 9 September 2008, 1688.
CB8	fd7	a. Hess, 7 March 1935, 67 = Ars Classica, 27–29 June 1928 XIII, 1332.
	fd8	a. UBS 75, 22 January 2008, 1049 = Künker 111, 18 March 2006, 6779 = UBS 63, 6 September 2005, 353 = UBS 62, 25 January 2005, 132.
		b. Ars Classica, 25 June 1924, manque.
	fd9	a. Tkalec and Astarte, 28 February 2007, 47 = Hess, 24 May 1935, 1735.
	fd21	a Lanz 36, April 1986, 705.
CB9	fd9	a. Lanz 123, 30 May 2005, 620.
		b. Bourgey, 16 December 1913, 313.
	fd11	a. Florange and Ciani, 18 December 1924, 389 = BM Card File, (no entry) 444.
CB10	fd6	a. NAC 52, 7 October 2009, 1126 = Münzhandlung Basel 8, 22 March 1937, 797.
		b. Ars Classica, 3 October 1934, 841.

c. BM 1964,1203.123 = Hess-Lucerne, 18 December 1933, 610 = Ars Classica, 12 June 1922, 952 = Hirsch, 11 May 1911, 1017.

d. Madrid 405 = Ratto, 12 May 1925, 1353.

e. Coin Galleries, 11 February 1988, 17.
f. Augsburg Hoard 47.

fd9   a. Leu 86, 5 May 2003, 867.

b. Ars Classica, October 1934 XVII, 840.
c. Page & Ciani, 1–10 April 1930, 161.
d. Vienna 36787.

CB11   fd6   a. Hess, 9 May 1951, 177.

fd10   a. Leu 93, 10 May 2005, 36.

b. Hess, 5 April 1955, 111 = M&M, 17–19 June 1954, 706 = Münzhandlung Basel, 15 March 1938, 652 = Hirsch, 23 May 1910, 744 = Sartiges 207.

c. Rollin & Feuardent, 20–28 April 1896, 404.
d. Paris 959.

fd17   a. Vinchon, 20 November 1992, 118 = Vinchon, 13 April 1991, 27.

CB12   fd6   a. M&M, 3–4 December 1948, 609.

fd7   a. *BMCRE* 1090.

b. Arquennes 731.

c. Leu, May 1986, 285.

d. Sternberg, May 1984, 352.
e. Leu, April 1975, 447.
f. Vinchon, June 1978, 140.
g. Trier 2450.

fd8   a. Hess-Lucerne, 18 December 1933, 609 = Ratto, 12 May 1925, 1352.

b. Vinchon, April 1976, 240.
c. Münzen und Medaillen, November 1970, 366.

fd10   a. NAC 52, 7 October 2009, 466 = NAC 46, 2 April 2008, 595.

b. Egger, 18 November 1912, 1228.

fd21   a. ANS 1958.223.13.

CB13   fd11   a. NAC 27, 12 May 2004, 418 = Ars Classica, 3 July 1933, 1863.

b. Ratto, 9 October 1934, 577 = Ars Classica, July 1930, 1662 = Rosenberg, 9 March 1914, 395 = Hirsch 12, 17 November 1904, 574.

c. Ratto, 7 February 1928, 3104 = BM Card File, key # 1114 (no entry), 3104 = Hirsch, 9 November 1910, 1092.

d. Vinchon, April 1988, 610 = Rollin & Feuardent, 20–28 April 1896, 406.

e. ANS 1958.223.4.

f. Arquennes 725.

g. Arquennes 726.

h. Münzen und Medaillen, November 1962, 618.

CB14	fd13	a. Stacks, 24 April 2008, 2309.

b. *BMCRE* 1089.

c. Hamburger, 29 May 1929, 619 = Ars Classica, 12 June 1922, 953.

d. Hess-Lucerne, 2 August 1933, 916 = Platt, 1932, 219.

e. Hirsch 18, 27 May 1907, 976.

f. CNG Triton III, 30 November 1999, 1098 = Hirsch, 13 November 1907, 607.

g. Schulman, 5 March 1923, 1634 = Sangiorgi, 15 April 1907, 1923.

h. Madrid 404.

i. Vienna 12434.

j. Berlin 18203628.

CB15	fd5	a. Ars Classica, 27–29 June 1928, 1333.
CB16	fd4	a. ANS 1944.100.81375.
	fd18	a. Ars Classica, 3 October 1934, 839 = Ars Classica, 3 July 1933, 1860.

b. Trier 2449.

CB17	fd2	a. ANS 1997.122.2 = Ars Classica, 3 October 1934, 842.

b. Bourgey, 10 December 1923, 229.

c. Glendining, 7–8 March 1957, 396.

CB19	fd10	a. Glendining, 25 November 1953, 179 = Santamaria, 29 March 1928, 179.

b. Hess-Leu, 14 April 1945, 315 = BM Card File, key #124 (no entry), 158.

c. CNG 39, 18 September 1996, 1491.

d. Arquennes 730.

e. Leu, May 1989, 359 = Leu, May 1985, 277.

	fd16	a. Christie's, June 1993, 146 = Ars Classica, 10 October 1938, 267.
	fd17	a. Hess-Leu, 2 April 1958, 342.

	fd19	a. Hirsch, 9 November 1910, 1091 = Sartiges 208.
		b. Paris 961. [die removed CB20 (=CB3)]
CB21	fd20	a. Feuardent, December 1921, 85. CB23 fd1 a. Hess, 9 May 1951, 178.
	fd9	a. ANS 1958.223.6.
		b. Madrid (rubbing 266). fd11a. ANS 1967.153.222.
		b Leu, May 1981, 465.
		c. Leu 36, May 1985, 276.
CB24	fd21	a. Hirsch 30, 17 November 1913, 1306.
	fd23	a. Vinchon, 22 November 1995, 101.
CB25	fd10	a. ANS 1958.223.14.
		b. Paris 960.
CB28	fd10	a. Paris, Armand Valton 1060.

VB   VENVS Venus standing l., holding apple in right hand, staff in left.

VB1	fd2	a. Künker 136, 10 March 2008, 1040 = NAC 34, 24 November 2006, 170 = NAC, 19 May 1999, 2061.
		b. Münzhandlung Basel 6, 18 March 1936, 1781.
		c. Madrid 408 = Ratto, 12 May 1925, 1377 = BM Card File, key #59 (no entry), 180.
		d. ANS 0000.999.20923.
		e. Trier 2457.
		f. Trier 2459.
VB3	fd2	a. Bourgey, 15 December 1924, 28.
		b. Trier 2458.
VB4	fd2	a. Lanz 148, 4 January 2010, 109.
		b. Ars Classica, 3 October 1934, 851 = Merzbacher, 15 November 1910, 1788.
		c. Hess, 6 January 1926, 1351.
		d. Baldwin's 6, 11 October 1995, 580 = ANS 1958.223.12.
		e. ANS 1997.122.1.
		f. Trier 2456.

VB5	fd2	a. Lanz 114, 26 May 2003, 411 = Lanz 106, 27 November 2001, 474 = Berk 17, 28 November 2000, 18 = Berk 115, 2 August 2000, 51.
		b. Arquennes 728.
		c. Arquennes 729.
VB6	fd1	a. *BMCRE* 1091.

Group V (fe) FAVSTINA AVGVSTA AVG PII F/FIL

VB   VENVS Venus standing l., holding apple in right hand, staff in left.

VB1	fe2	a. Arquennes 733.
	fe4	a. Glendining, 16–21 November 1950, 1550 = Canessa, 28 June 1923, 385 = Hirsch, 9 November 1910, 1096.
VB2	fe1	a. NAC K, 30 March 2000, 1854.
		b. Bourgey, 16 December 1913, 315.
	fe2	a. Vinchon, 15 November 1986, 68.
		b. NAC 52, 7 October 2009, 1127.
		c. *BMCRE* 1095.
		d. Ratto, 8 February 1928, 3135 = Hirsch, 27 November 1905, 1160.
		e. Santamaria, 29 November 1920, 796.
		f. Auctiones AG 26, 16–19 September 1996, 938.
		g. Christie's, 8 October 1985, 116.
		h. Arquennes 732.
		i. Paris 985.
VB3	fe2	a. Glendining, 27 September 1962, 200.
	fe3	a. Künker 104, 27 September 2005, 536 = Ars Classica, 3 October 1934, 850.
VB7	fe1	a. Trier 2460.
	fe2	a. BM Card File, key #3 (no entry), 57.
		b. Aureo, 11–12 December 1990, 75 = Aureo, 25 October 1989, 63.
VB8	fe4	a. Paris 986.
	fe2	a. Trier 2455.
VB9	fe4	a. Madrid (rubbing 268).
		b. Vienna 12510.

Group VI (ff) FAVSTINA AVGVSTA

Reverses have legend AVGVSTI PII FIL or descriptive legend.

AD Diana holding bow in l., arrow in r. hand.

AD1	ff1	a. NFA, 12 October 1988, 897 = Arquennes 734.
AD2	ff12[3]	a. Hess 257, November 1986, 346.
	ff2	a. Rauch 56, 5 February 1996, 3263.
		b. Leu 93, 10 May 2005, 37.
AD3	ff3	a. CNG Electronic Auction 196, 1 October 2008, 290.
		b. Trier 2438.
AD4	ff4	a. Rauch 85, 26 November 2009, 575 = Künker 155, 24 June 2009, 3024 = Lanz 145, 5 January 2009, 118.
		b. *BMCRE* 1096.
	ff11	a. Vinchon, 4–5 October 1989, 34.
		b. Vinchon, 9–10 June 2009, 35 = Vinchon, December 1983, 212.
		c. Heritage 3019, 26 April 2012, 23418.
AD5	ff5	a. Künker 97, 7 March 2005, 1469.
AD6	ff6	a. NAC 46, 2 April 2008, 594.
		b. Christie's, 10–11 October 1989, 197 = Christie's, 3–4 October 1988, 1199.
		c. Hess, April 1955, 112.
	ff8	a. Heritage 3042, 17 September 2015, 29218.
AD7	ff4	a. Peus 374, 23 April 2003, 772.
	ff7	a. NAC 24, 5 December 2002, 109.
		b. Paris 956.
		c. Leu, May 1974, 186.
		d. NAC 78, 26 May 2014, 999.
	ff8	a. BM 1964,1203.124.
		b. CNG 38, 6–7 June 1996, 1024.
		c. Rollin & Feuardent, 20–28 April 1896, 402.
		d. Trier 2437.

3. Obverse die ff12 has die damage at ST, not present on other ff12s.

AD8	ff5	a. UBS 64, 24 January 2006, 198.
		b. Trier 2443.
AD9	ff7	a. *BMCRE* 1097.
AD10	ff3	a. Robert Ball 39, April 1937, 1539.
	ff9	a. Aureo, 29 October 2002, 2250.
		b. Münzen und Medaillen, November/December 1982, 26.
		c. Trier 2439.
AD11	ff10	a. Christie's, 8 October 1985, 112.
		b. Schulman, June 1966, 1901.
AD12	ff12	a. ANS 1958.223.8.
		b. Trier 2446.
AD13	ff8	a. ANS 1958.223.7.
		b. Trier 2440.
AD14	ff8	a. Madrid (rubbing 264).
	ff9	a. CNG 99, 13 May 2015, 656.
	ff11	a. Paris 957.
		b. Trier 2442.
AD15	ff12	a. Paris 958.
		b. Trier 2444.
AD16	ff13	a. Vienna 12496.
	ff8	a. Vinchon, November 1986, 66.
AD17	ff14	a. Münzen und Medaillen, June 1964, 370.
AD18	ff5	a. Comptoir-des-monnaies, online sale November 2011.
		b. Roma Numismatics, 21 May 2013, 1446.
AD19	ff2	a. Trier 2441.
AD20	ff12	a. Trier 2445.
AD21	ff1	a. Trier 2447.

Die Catalogue, Part 2
Aurei of Faustina II under Marcus Aurelius

For an introduction to the catalogue format and the sources of the data (including abbreviations), see Die Catalogue Part 1.

Deleted dies:

fm62 deleted (= fm61) fm40 deleted (=fm27)

fm10, 35, 46, 52–56, 65, 67, 69, 70, 71 deleted (=denarius)

F1/fm49 deleted (Heritage 425, 6 January 2007, 50156) = denarius

NB: fm15 under Marcus Aurelius = ff3 under Antoninus Pius NB: fm6 under Marcus Aurelius = ff5 under Antoninus Pius

All obverse dies under Marcus Aurelius have the same legend format, which is also the same as the legend format "ff" under Antoninus Pius.

Summary of Reverse types and labels:

CC   CONCORDIA Concordia draped, seated l.

D   DIANA LVCIF Diana draped, standing l., holding lighted torch, transversely, pointing upwards to l., in both hands.

FA   FECVNDITATI AVGVSTAE Fecunditas seated r., holding child on lap; at her sides, two children standing.

FC   FECVND AVGVSTAE Fecunditas, draped, standing front, head l., holding child on each arm, two more children, l. and r., at her sides, stretching their arms up to her.

FE   FECVNDITATI AVGVSTAE Fecunditas (or Faustina II), diademed, standing r., holding child in arm: at her sides, two children standing.

H   HILARITAS Hilaritas, draped, standing l., holding long palm, nearly vertical, in r. hand and cornucopiae in l.

I   IVNO Juno, veiled, draped, standing l., holding patera in extended r. hand and vertical scepter in l.; at side, l., peacock standing, inclined l., head turned up to r.

IL   IVNONI LUCINAE Juno, draped, standing front, head l., holding child on l. arm and extending r. hand downwards; at her sides, two children, both standing l. and raising r. hands.

LA   LAETITIA Laetitia, draped, standing l., holding wreath in r. hand and scepter, nearly vertical, in l.

M   MATRI MAGNAE Cybele, towered, draped, seated r. on throne between two lions (the one on l. barely visible), holding drum balanced in l. hand on l. knee.

MC   MATRI CASTRORVM Female standing l., holding patera over lit altar, to the left two military standards.

SA   SALVTI AVGVSTAE Salus, draped, seated l. on throne, feeding snake coiled round altar out of patera in r. hand and resting l. elbow on arm of throne.

SF   SAECVLI FELIC Two infants seated on draped throne.

T   TEMPOR FELIC Felicitas, draped, standing front, head l., holding child on each arm: at sides, four children, two on r., two on l., all facing l.; the child on extreme l. extends both arms, the other three raise r. arms.

VE   VENVS Venus, draped, standing front, head r., holding apple in r. hand and vertical scepter in l.

VF   VENVS FELIX Venus, draped, seated l. on throne, holding three Graces in extended r. hand and vertical scepter in l.

VG   VENVS GENETRIX Venus, draped, standing front, head l., holding Victory in extended r. hand and resting l. hand on round shield, set on captive, seated front, with legs crossed.

VX   VENVS VICTRIX Venus, draped, standing front, head l., holding Victory in extended r. hand and resting l. on shield, set on helmet; she-wolf and twins on shield.

FAVSTINA AVGVSTA

CC   CONCORDIA Concordia, draped, seated l.

CC1   fm4   a. Aureo, 29 October 1991, 67.

b. NAC, 16 November 1994, 487 = Christie's, 9 October 1984, 76.

c. NAC 34, 24 November 2006, 30.

d. ANS 1958.223.9.

e. Vienna 36788.

D   DIANA LVCIF Diana, draped, standing l., holding lighted torch, transversely, pointing upwards to l., in both hands.

D1   fm6   a. Aureo, 5 April 1995, 135.

b. CNG 43, 24 September 1997, 2039.

c. BM Card File, key #250 (no entry), 239.

fm20   a. Vienna 36789.

D2   fm20   a. NAC K, 30 March 2000, 1856 = Christie's, 7 October 1986, 242.

b. Hess, 24 May 1935, 1737.

c. Hess-Leu, 14 April 1945, 316 = Rosenberg, 9 March 1914, 396.

d. ANS 1001.1.30019.

e. ANS 1958.223.16.

f. *BMCRE* 86.

g. Paris 963.

h. Trier 2479.

fm24   a. CNG Triton XIX, 5 January 2016, 573.

fm43   a. NFA 10, 17–18 September 1981, 354.

D3   fm24   a. Rollin & Feuardent, 20–28 April 1896, 407.

b. Ratto, 12 May 1925, 1358 = Ars Classica, 12 June 1922, 957.

c. Hess-Lucerne, 18 December 1933, 611.

d. Hess-Leu, April 1962, 479 = Hirsch, 6 May 1912, 1416 = Hirsch, 27 May 1907, 978 = BM Card File, key #350 (no entry), 49.

fm20   a. Künker 42, 13 March 1998, 3052 = Künker 34, 8–10 October 1996, 422.

b. Sambon Canessa, 18 November 1907, 2212.

                        c. Santamaria, 13 March 1953, 503.

D4   fm20   a. Hess 268, 23 October 1996, 36.

                        b. Santamaria, 24 January 1938, 617.

                        c. Arquennes 795.

D5   fm20   a. Baldwin's 48, 26 September 2006, 5010 = Hess-Leu, April 1968, 493.

                        b. Künker 124, 16 March 2007, 7642 = Auctiones, September 1981, 442.

                        c. Munzhandlung Basel, 22 March 1937, 801.

                        d. ANS 1959.228.1.

FA   FECVNDITATI AVGVSTAE Fecunditas seated r., holding child on lap; at her sides, two children standing.

FA1   fm2   a. Aureo, 11–12 December 1990, 72.

                        b. Vinchon, 11–13 April 1988, 611.

                        c. Hamburger, 25 October 1932, 916.

                        d. Page & Ciani, 1–10 April 1930, 162.

                fm47   a. CNG Triton VIII, 11 January 2005, 1150.

FA2   fm2   a. Christie's, 8 October 1985, 118.

                        b. UBS 75, 22 January 2008, 1058 = NFA Mail Bid 28, 23 April 1992, 1257 = NFA, 13 May 1991, 65 = CNG 5, 9 December 1988, 405 = Glendining, 16–21 November 1950, 1551 = Glendining, 27 May 1936, 180 = Schulman, 17 June 1924, 832 = Schulman, 5 March 1923, 1640 = Hirsch, 17 November 1913, 1309

                        c. Leu 53, 21–22 October 1991, 262.

                        d. M&M Basel 93, 16 December 2003, 185.

                        e. ANS 1955.191.16.

FC   FECVND AVGVSTAE Fecunditas, draped, standing front, head l., holding child on each arm, two more children, l. and r., at her sides, stretching their arms up to her.

FC1   fm72   a. NAC 49, 21 October 2008, 283.

FC2   fm72   a. NAC 84, 20 May 2015, 1910.

FE   **FECVNDITATI AVGVSTAE Fecunditas (or Faustina II), diademed, standing r., holding child in arm; at her sides, two children standing.**

     FE1   fm15   a. Vinchon, 17 November 1990, 57 = Christie's, 9 October 1984, 77

                              = Bourgey, 16 May 1914, 231.

             fm32   a. Cahn, 3 November 1913, 457.

             fm2   a. Platt, 1930, 1116.

                          b. Ciani, 7 May 1955, 356 = Feuardent, 16 June 1924, 217 = BM Card File, key #41 (no entry), 546.

     FE2   fm38   a. Lanz 82, 24 November 1997, 393 = Sotheby's, July 1996, 126.

     FE3   fm15   a. Ars Classica, 3 July 1933, 1867.

                          b. ANS 1958.223.10.

     FE4   fm15   a. BM Card File, key #124 (no entry), 159.

                          b. Arquennes 796.

                          c. Vienna 12421.

H   **HILARITAS Hilaritas, draped, standing l., holding long palm, nearly vertical, in r. hand and cornucopiae in l.**

     H1   fm13   a. Coin Galleries, 27 February 2001, 12 = Bourgey, 4–5 June 1991, 260 = Rollin & Feuardent, 20–28 April 1896, 408.

                          b. Ars Classica, 3 July 1933, 1868.
                          c. Ars Classica, 3 October 1934, 844.
                          d. Ratto, 12 May 1925, 1362 = Bourgey, 7–9 December 1908, 455.

                          e. Ciani, 12 December 1935, 21.
                          f. Egger, 15 January 1912, 1024.
                          g. Hess, 24 May 1935, 1738.

                          h. Madrid (rubbing 261).
                          i. Vienna 12454.
                          j. Trier 2480.

             fm14   a. Bourgey, 21–22 January 1992, 146.

                          b. ANS 1944.100.49230.

             fm17   a. Arquennes 797.

     H2   fm17   a. Christie's, 8 October 1985, 119.

                              b. Niggeler, 3 November 1967, 1327 = Helbing, 20 March 1928, 553.

          c. Vinchon, December 1975, 220.

	fm39	a. Münzen & Medaillen 95, 4 October 2004, 148.
H3	fm13	a. Peus 413, 29 October 2014, 352.
	fm25	a. NAC, 18 May 2000, 560.
H4	fm13	a. Künker 111, 18 March 2006, 6804.
		b. BM Card File, key #1911 (no entry), 1615.
		c. Schulman, 5 March 1923, 1641.
H5	fm25	a. *BMCRE* 98.
	fm33	a. Ars Classica, 12 June 1922, 963 = Feuardent, 2 April 1914, 401 = Bourgey, 16 December 1913, 2930. b. *BMCRE* 99.
H6	fm14	a. Adolf Hess, 9 May 1951, 179.
H7	fm 14	a. Trier 2481.

I   **IVNO Juno, veiled, draped, standing l., holding patera in extended r. hand and vertical scepter in l.; at side, l., peacock standing, inclined l., head turned up to r.**

I1	fm25	a. Rollin & Feuardent, 20–28 April 1896, 409.

IL   **IVNONI LUCINAE Juno, draped, standing front, head l., holding child on l. arm and extending r. hand downwards; at her sides, two children, both standing l. and raising r. hands.**

IL1	fm26	a. Canessa, 28 June 1923, 379 = Hirsch, 23 May 1910, 747 = Rollin & Feuardent, 20–28 April 1896, 410.
IL2	fm42	a. NAC C, 11–12 March 1993, 1864 = Sotheby's (Met Sale), November 1972, 324. b. BM Card File, key #45 (no entry), 1518. c. ANS 1001.1.30118. d. *BMCRE* 116. e. NFA, March 1975, 362. f. Berlin 18203689.

	fm61	a. Adolf Hess, 9 May 1951, 181.
	fm77	a. Sotheby's (Met Sale), November 1972, 325.
IL3	fm61	a. Helbing, 31 January 1930, 1210.
IL4	fm63	a. Hess, 24 May 1935, 1739.
IL5	fm64	a. Münzen & Medaillen, 13–14 January 1953, 363.
IL6	fm72	a. Madrid 430.
IL7	fm42	a. Arquennes 798.
	fm61	a. *BMCRE* 117.
IL8	fm80	a. Brussels, Coll. du Chastel 622.

LA   LAETITIA Laetitia, draped, standing l., holding wreath in r. hand and scepter, nearly vertical, in l.

LA1	fm7	a. Stack's Bowers and Ponterio Sale 174, 12 January 2013, 2053.
	fm16	a. Christie's, 9 October 1984, 78.
	fm27	b. ANS 1959.228.2.

M   MATRI MAGNAE Cybele, towered, draped, seated r. on throne between two lions (the one on l. barely visible), holding drum balanced in l. hand on l. knee.

M1	fm5	a. CNG 54, 14 June 2000, 1624 = CNG Triton 3, 30 November 1999, 1099 = NAC 6, 11 March 1993, 448 = Aureo, 31 March 1992, 67.
		b. Goldberg 47, 25 May 2008, 1296 = NFA/Leu, 16 May 1984 (Garrett Coll. I), 814.
		c. *BMCRE* 132.
M2	fm5	a. Christie's, 9 October 1984, 79.
		b. Leu 54, 28 April 1992, 258.
	fm31	a. Leu 52, 15 May 1991, 211.
		b. Vinchon, 15 November 1986, 67.
		c. Künker 124, 16 March 2007, 7643.
	fm51	a. *BMCRE* 133.
M3	fm21	a. Coin Galleries, 14 November 1984, 14.
M4	fm21	a. Rollin & Feuardent, 20–28 April 1896, 412.
M5	fm31	a. NAC 38, 21 March 2007, 78 = Hess 257, 12 November 1986, 348.
		b. Vinchon, 14–15 December 1999, 734.

	fm21	a. UBS 75, 22 January 2008, 1057.
M6	fm44	a. NFA 10, 17–18 September 1981, 355 = ANS 1959.228.35.
		b. ANS 1944.100.81376.
		c. ANS 1959.228.3.
	fm51	a. Leu 93, 10 May 2005, 38 = NFA 1975, 361.
	fm76	a. Münzen und Medaillen 7, December 1948, 612.
M7	fm5	a. Rauch 76, 17 October 2005, 545.
	fm76	a. Leu, April 1972, 410.

MC   **MATRI CASTRORVM Female standing l., holding patera over lit altar, to the left two military standards.**

MC1   fm81   a. Brussels, Coll. du Chastel 34.

SA   **SALVTI AVGVSTAE Salus, draped, seated l. on throne, feeding snake coiled round altar out of patera in r. hand and resting l. elbow on arm of throne.**

SA1   fm1   a. Titano 72, 1 March 1998, 247 = Rauch 56, 5 February 1996, 3264.

                b. ANS 1944.100.49239.

SA2   fm3   a. Aureo, 30 June 1992, 27 = Aureo, 11–12 December 1990, 74 = Aureo, 12 January 1990, 85 = Arquennes 799.

                b. Schulman, 6 June 1930, 351 = Bourgey, 4–5 November 1913, 351.

SA3   fm7   a. Aureo, 29 October 2002, 2251 = Arquennes 802.

                b. Vinchon, 15 November 1989, 150 = Vinchon 7, 9–10 December 1983, 213.

                c. Vinchon, 30 November – 1 December 1996, 39.

                d. Künker 20, 30 September – 2 October 1991, 624.

                e. Peus 371, 24 April 2002, 417 = Peus 369, 31 October 2001, 594.

                f. NAC 25, 25 June 2003, 485.

                g. Ars Classica, 25 June 1924, 1059.

                h. Ars Classica, 3 October 1934, 848 = Ars Classica, 18 October 1926, 2932.

                i. Canessa, 28 June 1923, 380.

                j. Glendining, 24 November 1925, 119.

k. Hess, 24 May 1935, 1740.

l. Hirsch, 23 May 1910, 750.

m. Hirsch, 17 November 1913, 1315.

n. Bourgey, 12 November 1951, 36.

o. Trier 2483.

fm9   a. Feuardent, 2 April 1914, 404.

fm19   a. Platt, 27 June 1925, 200.

b. Arquennes 800.

fm48   a. Arquennes 803.

SA4   fm9   a. Aureo Jueves, 28 October 1993, 49 = Christie's, 13 October 1992, 607.

b. Schulman, 5 March 1923, 1654.

c. Schulman, 9 October 1933, 93.

d. Vienna 36791.

fm12   a. ANS 1959.228.4.

fm28   a. Vinchon, 15 November 1989, 151 = Vinchon 7, 9–10 December 1983, 214.

b. ANS 1959.228.6.

SA5   fm11   a. Bourgey, 4–5 May 1987, 117.

b. Heidelberger 51, 19–20 May 2009, 114 = Künker 124, 16 March 2007, 7644.

c. Art Coins Roma, 31 May 2011, 376 = Lanz 125, 28 November 2005, 797 = Florange and Ciani, 28 May 1924, 63.

d. Glendining, 27 May 1936, 182 = Bourgey, 29 May 1911, 536.

e. Glendining, 20 February 1951, 1802.

f. Munzhandlung Basel, 22 March 1937, 804.

SA6   fm12   a. Bourgey, 2–4 June 1988, 166.

fm19   a. Ars Classica, 3 July 1933, 1876.

b. Ars Classica, 3 July 1933, 1879.

c. Adolf Hess, 9 May 1951, 182.

d. Schulman, 27 February 1939, 62.

SA7   fm18   a. Christie's, 8 October 1985, 120.

SA8   fm7   a. Hess 257, 12 November 1986, 349 = Apostolo Zeno, 8–9 June 1956, 381 = Glendining, 14 January 1953, 51 = Hess, 24 May 1935, 240 = Merzbacher, 15 November 1910, 1784 = Egger, 28 November 1905, 2515 = BM Card File, (no entry), 381.

                        b. Santamaria, 25 May 1926, 521 = Santamaria, 16 January 1924, 476.

                        c. Arquennes 801.

                        d. Vienna 12497.

                        e. Berlin 18204945.

fm19 a. Christie's, 7 October 1986, 188.

      b. Vinchon, 24–25 November 1994, 345.

      c. Vinchon, 24–26 April 1996, 72 = Bourgey, December 1922, 31.

      d. Ciani, 12 December 1935, 22.

      e. Bourgey, 6–7 December 1961, 61.

      f. Glendining, 16–21 November 1950, 1549.

      g. Page & Ciani, 14 June 1934, 209.

fm34 a. Künker 29, 8–10 March 1995, 2226.

SA9   fm22 a. Coin Galleries, 10 April 1991, 23.

      b. CNG Mail Bid 57, 4 April 2001, 1291.

      c. Bourgey, 10 December 1923, 231.

      d. Ars Classica, 3 October 1934, 849.

fm29 a. Vinchon 2, 17–18 December 1996, 191 = Vinchon, 22–23 May 1995, 339.

      b. Riechmann, 18 September 1922, 727.

SA10   fm7 a. Spink 4026, 15 April 2004, 41 = BM Card File, key #283 (no entry), 563.

fm16 a. Auctiones, November 1974, 346.

fm19 a. Künker 112, 20 June 2006, 1015 = Künker 104, 27 September 2005, 545.

fm23 a. Noble 93, 13 May 2010, 4860 = Coin Galleries, 14 December 2004, 44 = Coin Galleries, 25 February 2004, 13.

SA11   fm27 a. Rollin & Feuardent, 20–28 April 1896, 413.

      b. Cahn, 27 February 1933, 765.

      c. Canessa, 28 June 1923, 381.

      d. ANS 1959.228.34.

      e. Arquennes 805.

      f. Trier 2485.

fm41 a. NAC B, 25–26 February 1992, 1971.

      b. Ars Classica, 3 October 1934, 847.

                        c. Schlesinger, 31 January – 1 February 1938, 560.

          fm73   a. Madrid (rubbing 262).

SA12   fm18   a. Rollin & Feuardent, 20–28 April 1896, 414.

                        b. Künker 42, 13 March 1998, 3053.

                        c. Trier 2487.

          fm37   a. Lanz 42, 23 November 1987, 558 = Aufhaeuser, 2 October 1985, 272.

          fm8   a. Ars Classica, 25 June 1924, 1060.

                        b. Helbing, 20 June 1929, 4259.

                        c. Helbing, 31 January 1930, 491.

                        d. Hirsch, 23 May 1910, 751.

SA13   fm11   a. Vinchon, 20 November 1992, 119.

                        b. Florange and Ciani, 18 December 1924, 390 = Bourgey 36, 14 December 1911, 98.
                        c. BM Card File, (no entry), 118.

                        d. Schulman, 18 December 1926, 266.

                        e. Schulman, 7 June 1937, 272.

          fm59   a. Monnaies, 27 June 1925, 226.

SA14   fm22   a. Hess 257, 12 November 1986, 350.

SA15   fm36   a. Lanz 40, 25 May 1987, 695.

SA16   fm36   a. NAC 64, 17 May 2012, 1201 = Lanz 94, 22 November 1999, 624.

                        b. Trier 2484.

SA17   fm27   a. NAC, 26–27 October 1995, 618 = Ars Classica, 3 October 1934, 846.

SA18   fm11   a. NAC H, 30 April 1998, 2033.

                        b. Rauch 82, 23 April 2008, 371 = Spink 5014, 28 September 2005, 444.

          fm60   a. BM Card File, key #62 (no entry), 1595.

                        b. Arquennes 804.

SA19   fm1   a. Santamaria, 29 November 1920, 795.

          fm12   a. Hess-Divo 314, 4 May 2009, 1570.

          fm19   a. NAC K, 30 March 2000, 1857.

                        b. Bourgey, 10 December 1923, 230.

                        c. Glendining, 27 September 1962, 201.

          fm45   a. Hess-Divo 309, 28 April 2008, 168 = NAC 31, 26 October 2005, 58 = NFA 14, 29 November 1984, 440.

b. Trier 2489.

SA 20   fm22   a. Gorny & Mosch 146, 6 March 2006, 469 = Peus 369, 31 October 2001, 593.

b. Ars Classica, 3 July 1933, 1880.

SA21   fm48   a. Künker 133, 11 October 2007, 8916 = Künker 111, 18 March 2006, 6805.

b. Glendining, 7–8 March 1957, 398.
c. Hess-Leu, 4 April 1963, 195.

d. *BMCRE* 152.

SA22   fm27   a. NAC 34, 24 November 2006, 31.

SA23   fm1   a. Feuardent, 18 June 1924, 1218.

fm74   a. *BMCRE* 153.

SA24   fm36   a. Ars Classica, 3 July 1933, 1875.

b. Berlin 18204946.

fm75   a. Hess-Leu 1957, 357.

SA25   fm7   a. Ars Classica, 3 July 1933, 1877.

b. *BMCRE* 151.

fm19   a. Madrid 433.

SA26   fm27   a. Ars Classica, 3 October 1934, 845 = Ars Classica, 3 July 1933, 1878.

b. Hess-Leu, 2 April 1958, 344.

fm60   a. Schulman, 6 June 1930, 454.

b. Via Po 376.

fm68   a. Santamaria, 24 January 1938, 621.

SA27   fm57   a. Glendining, 7–8 March 1957, 399.

b. ANS 1959.228.5.

SA28   fm58   a. Glendining, 27 May 1941, 544 = Sotheby's, 25 March 1935, 84 = Glendining-Seaby, 15 July 1929, 839.

SA29   fm3   a. Leu 91, 10–11 May 2004, 573 = Münzen & Medaillen, 17–19 June 1954, 707.

SA30   fm36   a. Leu 72, 12 May 1998, 455 = Leu, May 1973, 390 = Hess-Leu, 4 April 1963, 196.

SA31   fm7   a. Münzen & Medaillen, 3–4 December 1948, 614

SA32   fm22   a. Arquennes 806.

SA33   fm18   a. *BMCRE* 154.

b. Trier 2488.

SA34   fm41   a. Auctiones, June 1977, 705.

SA35   fm22   a. Trier 2486.

SF   **SAECVLI FELIC Two infants seated on draped throne.**

SF1   fm79   a. Trier 2482.

T   **TEMPOR FELIC Felicitas, draped, standing front, head l., holding child on each arm; at sides, four children, two on r., two on l., all facing l.; the child on extreme l. extends both arms, the other three raise r. arms.**

T1   fm8   a. Aureo, 21 June 2007, 51.

b. Madrid (rubbing 263).

T2   fm8   a. *BMCRE* 155.

VE   **VENVS Venus, draped, standing front, head r., holding apple in r. hand and vertical scepter in l.**

VE1   fm30   a. Vinchon Salell, 9–10 June 2009, 36.

b. No Entry, July 1993, No Lot.

VE2   fm30   a. Ars Classica, 3 July 1933, 1888 = Ars Classica, 27–29 June 1929, 1342.

VE3   fm66   a. Canessa, 28 June 1923, 386.

b. Egger, 15 January 1912, 1033.

VF   **VENVS FELIX Venus, draped, seated l. on throne, holding three Graces in extended r. hand and vertical scepter in l.**

VF1   fm50   a. Hess-Divo 308, 24 October 2007, 218.

VF2   fm78   a. NAC 52, 7 October 2009, 470.

VG   **VENVS GENETRIX Venus, draped, standing front, head l., holding Victory in extended r. hand and resting l. hand on round shield, set on captive, seated front, with legs crossed.**

    VG1   fm27   a. *BMCRE* 171.

VX   **VENVS VICTRIX Venus, draped, standing front, head l., holding Victory in extended r. hand and resting l. on shield, set on helmet; she-wolf and twins on shield.**

    VX1   fm4   a. Vinchon, 30 June 1978, 141.

              fm14   a. Ars Classica, 10 October 1938, 270.

                       b. Canessa, 28 June 1923, 387.
                       c. Sartiges 209.
                       d. Hirsch, 9 November 1910, 1098.
                       e. ANS 1958.223.11.

                       f. *BMCRE* 174.

                       g. Leu, May 1977, 342.

    VX2   fm14   a. ANS 1955.191.17.

                       b. Münzen und Medaillen, April 1963, 60.

                       c. Leu 33, May 1983, 73.

Key to the Die Link Charts

Linked dies are arranged in chains (long sequences with many dies and often a clear chronological order), groups (short sequences where no chronological order can be determined), and pairs (paired obverse and reverse dies that do not link to larger groups or chains). Most of these are illustrated as figures in the individual chapters of this book. The others, which were not included in the chapter figures because they do not contribute extra information to the subjects discussed there, are illustrated in the die link charts at the end of the book. The following key references the specific location where the relevant die link chart may be found. The die link charts were initially assembled and labeled some years ago. Over time, as new data was collected and added to the study, some groups and pairs were found to link into other, larger groups and chains. When these were merged with the larger group or chain, their number was simply removed from the sequence without renumbering the other groups or pairs in the overall sequence. This was done to avoid potential errors in extensive renumbering. The merged groups and pairs are indicated in the list below.

Chain 1 - Figs. 2.1 and 2.8
      2 - Fig. 3.1
      3 - Fig. 3.7
      4 - Fig. 4.1
      5 - Fig. 4.2 partial view only, full view in Charts 2 and 3
      6 - Fig. 4.2 partial view only, full view in Chart 4
      7 - Fig. 4.9 partial view only, full view in Charts 6 and 7
      8 - Fig. 4.10
      9 - Fig. 4.10

Group 1 - Chart 1
        [2 - merged]
        3 - Chart 1
        4-9 - Fig. 3.6
        10-11 - Chart 5
        12-15 - Fig. 4.4
        16-17 - Chart 8
        18 - Fig. 4.10

Pair 1-2 - Chart 1
        3 - Fig. 3.6
        4 - Chart 5
        [5 - merged]
        6 - Chart 5
        [7 - merged]
        8-10 - Chart 5
        [11 - merged]
        12 and 12a - Chart 5
        13 - Fig. 4.4
        14-16 - Chart 8
        17-19 - Fig. 4.12

* These charts only illustrate the chains, groups, and pairs not illustrated in the main text.

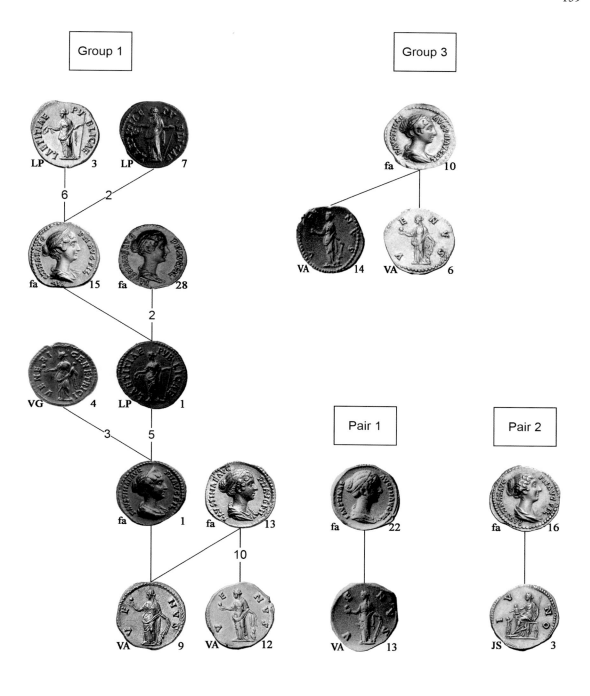

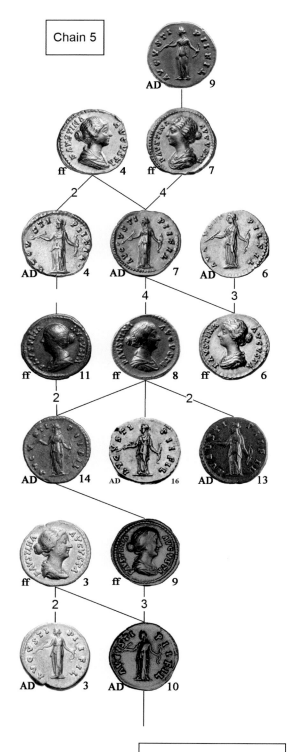

continued next chart

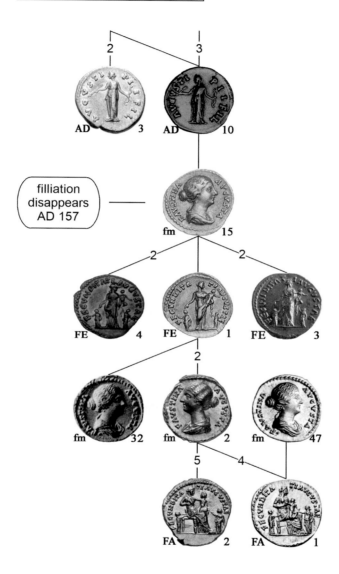

Chain 5 (continued)

2   3

AD 3   AD 10

filliation disappears AD 157

fm 15

2   2

FE 4   FE 1   FE 3

2

fm 32   fm 2   fm 47

5   4

FA 2   FA 1

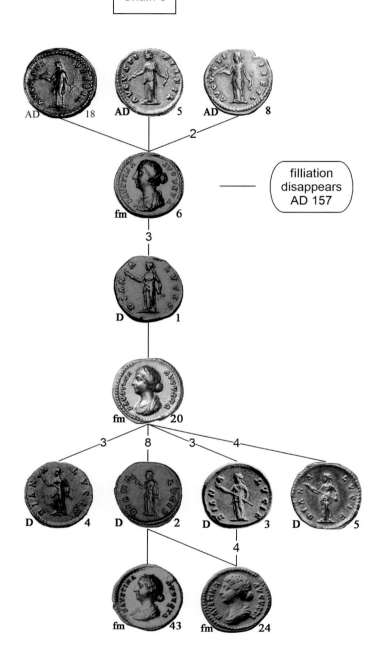

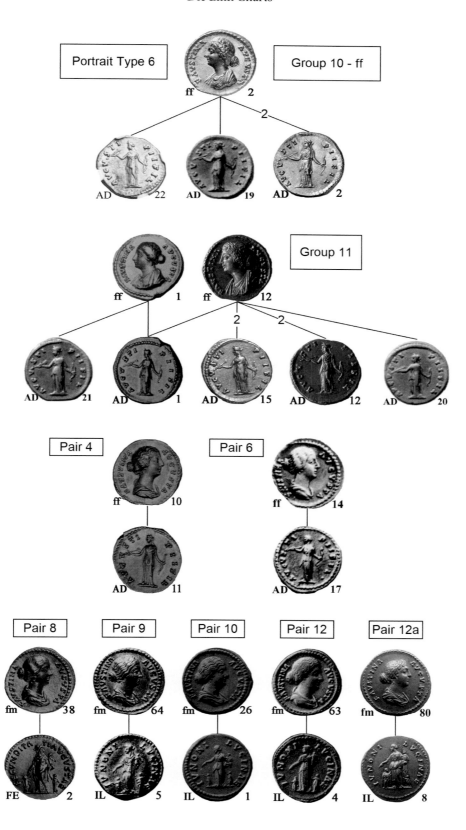

Portrait Type 6

Group 10 - ff

ff 2

AD 22
AD 19
AD 2

Group 11

ff 1
ff 12

AD 21
AD 1
AD 15
AD 12
AD 20

Pair 4

Pair 6

ff 10

ff 14

AD 11

AD 17

Pair 8
Pair 9
Pair 10
Pair 12
Pair 12a

fm 38
fm 64
fm 26
fm 63
fm 80

FE 2
IL 5
IL 1
IL 4
IL 8

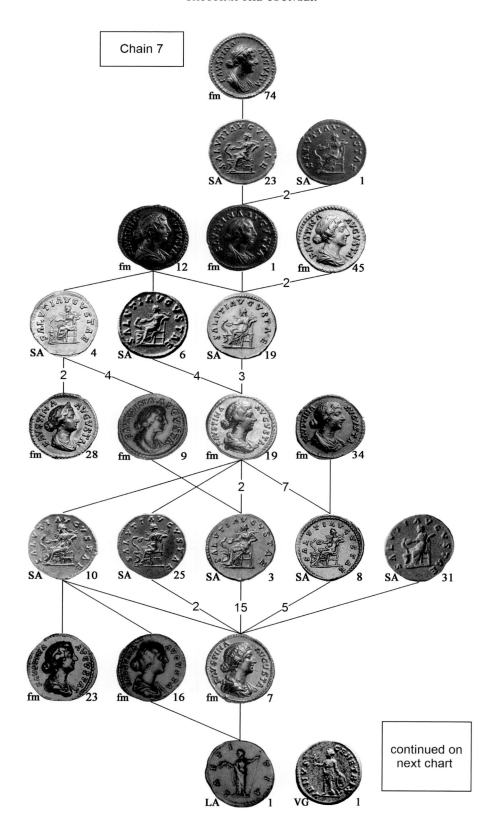

Chain 7

fm 74

SA 23   SA 1

2

fm 12   fm 1   fm 45

2

SA 4   SA 6   SA 19

2   4   4   3

fm 28   fm 9   fm 19   fm 34

2   7

SA 10   SA 25   SA 3   SA 8   SA 31

2   15   5

fm 23   fm 16   fm 7

LA 1   VG 1

continued on next chart

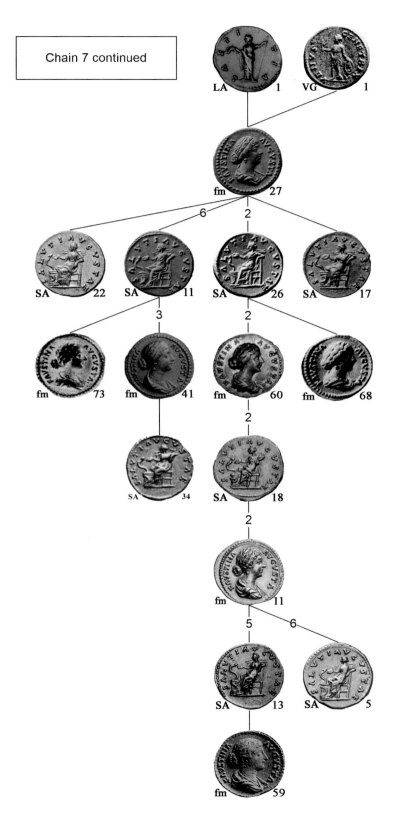

Chain 7 continued

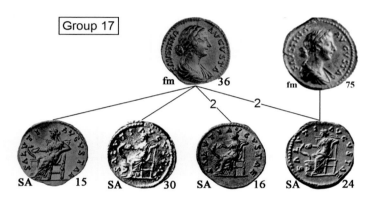

List of Die Illustrations

The following key indicates in short form the sources of the images used to illustrate each die in the die link chats. The identifications are limited to the name of the collection, hoard or auction house and the catalogue or lot number of the coin. To find the exact auction date, it will be necessary to look up the relevant entry in the catalogue.

OBVERSE DIES, ANTONINUS PIUS

fa1 Hess 347
fa2 NAC 467
fa3 NAC 169
fa4 NAC 57
fa5 Vinchon 340
fa6 Tkalec 236
fa7 Baldwins 179
fa8 CNG 1290
fa9 NAC 103
fa10 CNG 1023
fa11 M&M 146
fa12 Kuenker 535
fa13 Leu 865
fa14 Leu 34
fa15 NAC 130
fa16 NAC 1091
fa17 NAC 484

fa18 NAC 505
fa19 BMCRE 1044
fa20 Christies 117
fa21 Feuardent 405
fa22 Bourgey 232
fa23 ANS 1966.62.20
fa24 Glendining 116
fa25 Paris 962
fa26 Hess-Lucerne 622
fa27 M&M 709
fa28 Christies 115
fc1 Kuenker 7637
fc2 M&M 184
fc3 Ars Classica 1487
fc4 Christies 74
fc5 Christies 114
fc6 Vinchon 120

fd1 M&M 147
fd2 NAC 170
fd3 Vinchon 35
fd4 CNG 1378
fd5 Goldberg 1904
fd6 BMCRE 1964.1203.123
fd7 Kuenker 3023
fd8 Kuenker 6779
fd9 Lanz 620
fd10 Leu 36
fd11 NAC 418
fd12 Peus 579
fd13 BMCRE 1089
fd14 UBS 1688
fd15 BMCRE 1084
fd16 Ars Classica 1862
fd17 Hess-Leu 342
fd18 Ars Classica 1860
fd19 Paris 961
fd20 Feuardent 85

fd21 Hirsch 1306
fd22 CNG 1537
fd23 Vinchon 101
fe1 NAC 1854
fe2 Vinchon 68
fe3 Kuenker 536
fe4 Paris 986
ff1 NFA 897
ff2 Leu 37
ff3 CNG 290
ff4 Kuenker 3024
ff5 Kuenker 1469
ff6 NAC 594
ff7 NAC 109
ff8 BMCRE 1964.1203.124
ff9 Aureo 2250
ff10 Christies 112
ff11 Paris 957
ff12 ANS 1958.223.8
ff13 ANS 1958.223.16

REVERSE DIES, ANTONINUS PIUS

AD1 NFA 897
AD2 Leu 37
AD3 CNG 290
AD4 Kuenker 3024
AD5 Kuenker 1469
AD6 NAC 594
AD7 NAC 109
AD8 UBS 198
AD9 BMCRE 1097
AD10 Aureo 2250
AD11 Christies 112
AD12 ANS 1958.223.8
AD13 ANS 1958.223.7
AD14 Paris 957
AD15 Paris 958
C1 Kuenker 7637
C2 Peus 579
C3 BMCRE 1041

C4 Feuardent 403
C5 Vinchon 64
CB1 CNG 1494
CB2 NAC 380
CB3 Vinchon 35
CB4 CNG 1378
CB5 Goldberg 1904
CB6 Hess 1568
CB7 Kuenker 3023
CB8 Kuenker 6779
CB9 Lanz 620
CB10 Leu 867
CB11 Leu 36
CB12 NAC 595
CB13 NAC 418
CB14 BMCRE 1089
CB15 Ars Classica 1333
CB16 Ars Classica 1860

OBVERSE DIES, MARCUS AURELIUS

fm1 ANS 1944.100.49239

fm2 Munzen 185

fm3 Aureo 85 au

fm4 Numismatica 30

fm5 Goldberg 1296

fm6 CNG 2039

fm7 Numismatica 485

fm8 Ars Classica 1060

fm9 Aureo Jueves 49

fm10 Baldwin 581

fm11 Lanz 797

fm12 ANS 1959.228.4

fm13 Rollin 408

fm14 ANS 1944.100.49230

fm15 Vinchon 57

fm16 Christie's 78

fm17 Christie's 119

fm18 Rollin 414

fm19 Fritz 1015

fm20 Fritz 7642

fm21 UBS 1057

fm22 Gorny 269

fm23 Coin Galleries 13

fm24 Rollin 407

fm25 BMCRE 98

fm26 Rollin 410

fm27 Rollin 413

fm28 Vinchon 151

fm29 Vinchon No Lot

fm30 Ars Classica 1342

fm31 Fritz 7643

fm32 Cahn 457

fm33 Feuardent 401

fm34 Kunker 2226

fm35 Ball 1691

fm36 Lanz 695

fm37 Lanz 558

fm38 Lanz 393

fm39 Muenz 148

fm40 Numismatica 31

fm41 NAC 1971

fm42 BMCRE 116

fm43 NFA 354

fm44 ANS 1959.228.3

fm45 Numismatica 58

fm46 Rauch 303

fm47 Classical Numismatic 1150

fm48 Fritz 8916

fm49 Heritage 50156

fm50 Hess-Divo 318

fm51 Leu 38

fm52 Baranowsky 733

fm53 Ratto 582

fm54 Munzenhandlung 1782

fm55 Hess 1745

fm56 Hess 612

fm57 ANS 1959.228.5

fm58 Glendining 839

fm59 Monnaies 226

fm60 Arquenes 804

fm61 BMCRE 117

fm62 Helbing 1210

fm63 Hess 1739

fm64 Munzen 363

fm65 Bourgey 233

fm66 Egger 1033

fm67 BM photo file No Entry 1690

fm68 Santamaria 621

fm69 Santamaria 71

fm70 Munzhandlung 1785

fm71 Christies 610

fm72 Madrid 430

fm73 Madrid rubbing 262

fm74 BMCRE 153

REVERSE DIES, MARCUS AURELIUS

CC1 Numismatica 30
D1 CNG 2039
D2 Christie's 242
D3 Hirsch 1416
D4 Hess 36
D5 Baldwin 5010
F1 Heritage 50156
FA1 Classical Numismatic 1150
FA2 Munzen 185
FE1 Vinchon 57
FE2 Lanz 393
FE3 ANS 1958.223.10
FE4 Arquenes 796
FO1 Baranowsky 733
FO2 Baranowsky 2124
FO3 Cahn 760
FO4 Hess 1745
H1 Rollin 408
H2 Muenz 148
H3 NAC 560
H4 Fritz 6804
H5 BMCRE 98
H6 Adolf Hess 179
I1 Rollin 409
IL1 Rollin 410
IL2 BMCRE 116
IL3 Helbing 1210
IL4 Hess 1739
IL5 Munzen 363
IL6 Madrid 430
IL7 Arquenes 798
IO1 Hess 612
IR1 Rauch 303
LA1 Christie's 78
M1 Goldberg 1296
M2 Fritz 7643
M3 Coin Galleries 14
M4 Rollin 412
M5 UBS 1057
M6 Leu 38

M7 Rauch 545
M8 Madrid 431
S1 Ball 1691
S2 Bourgey 233
S3 Glendining 118
S4 Munzhandlung 1785
S5 No Entry 1690
S6 Santamaria 71
SA1 ANS 1944.100.49239
SA2 Aureo 85
SA3 Numismatica 485
SA4 Vinchon 151
SA5 Fritz 7644
SA6 Ars Classica 1879
SA7 Christie's 120
SA8 Vinchon 72
SA9 Classical Numismatic 1291
SA10 Spink 41
SA11 Rollin 413
SA12 Lanz 558
SA13 Vinchon 119
SA14 Hess 350
SA15 Lanz 695
SA16 Lanz 624
SA17 NAC 618
SA18 Rauch 371
SA19 Numismatica 58
SA20 Gorny 269
SA21 Fritz 8916
SA22 Numismatica 31
SA23 BMCRE 153
SA24 Ars Classica 1875
SA25 BMCRE 151
SA26 Ars Classica 1878
SA27 ANS 1959.228.5
SA28 Glendining 544
SA29 Munzen 707
SA30 Hess 196
SA31 Munzen 614
SA32 Arquenes 806

SA33 BMCRE 154
SF1 Baldwin 581
SF2 Christies 610
T1 Aureo 51
T2 BMCRE 155
VE1 BM photo file No Entry No Lot

VE2 Ars Classica 1342
VE3 Egger 1033
VF1 Hess-Divo 318
VG1 BMCRE 171
VX1 Vinchon 141
VX2 ANS 1955.191.17

Plates

ANTONINUS PIUS: OBVERSES

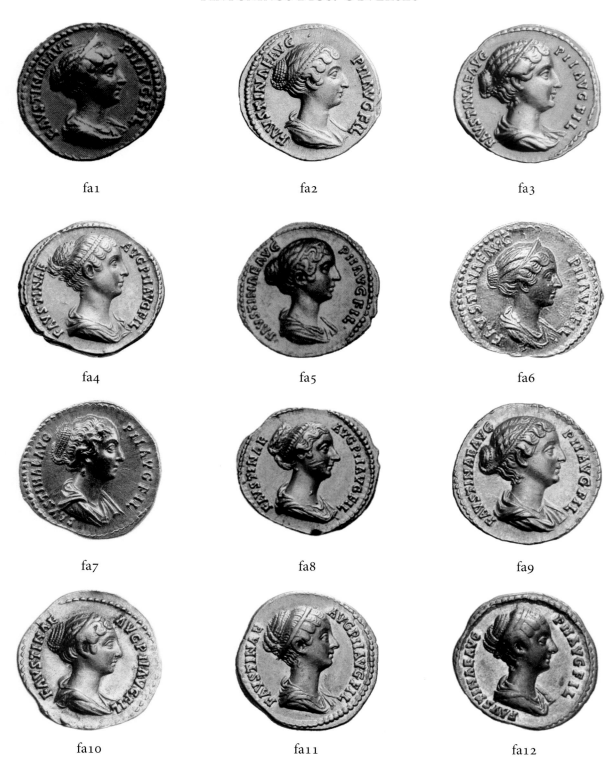

fa1

fa2

fa3

fa4

fa5

fa6

fa7

fa8

fa9

fa10

fa11

fa12

fa13   fa14   fa15

fa16   fa17   fa18

fa19   fa20   fa21

fa22   fa23   fa25

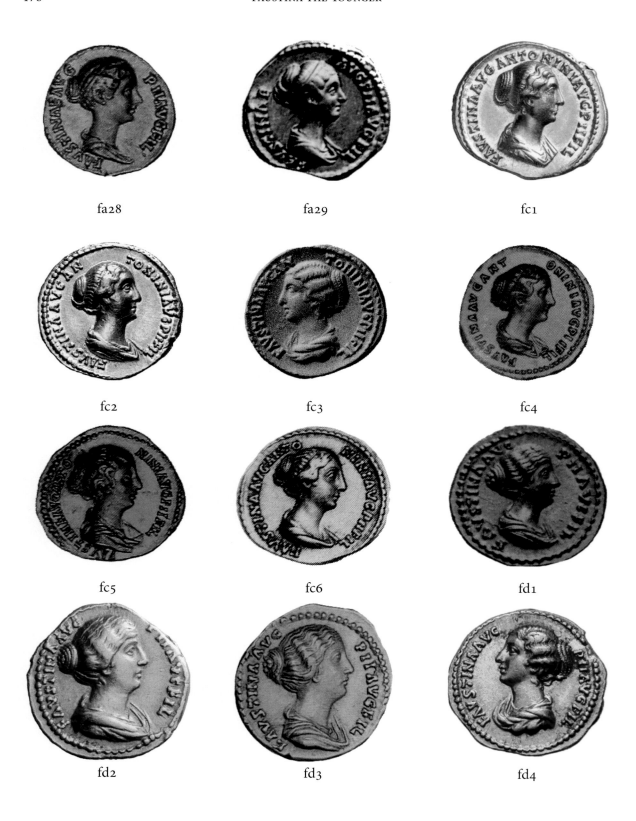

fa28

fa29

fc1

fc2

fc3

fc4

fc5

fc6

fd1

fd2

fd3

fd4

fd5 fd6 fd7

fd8 fd9 fd10

fd11 fd12 fd13

fd14 fd15 fd16

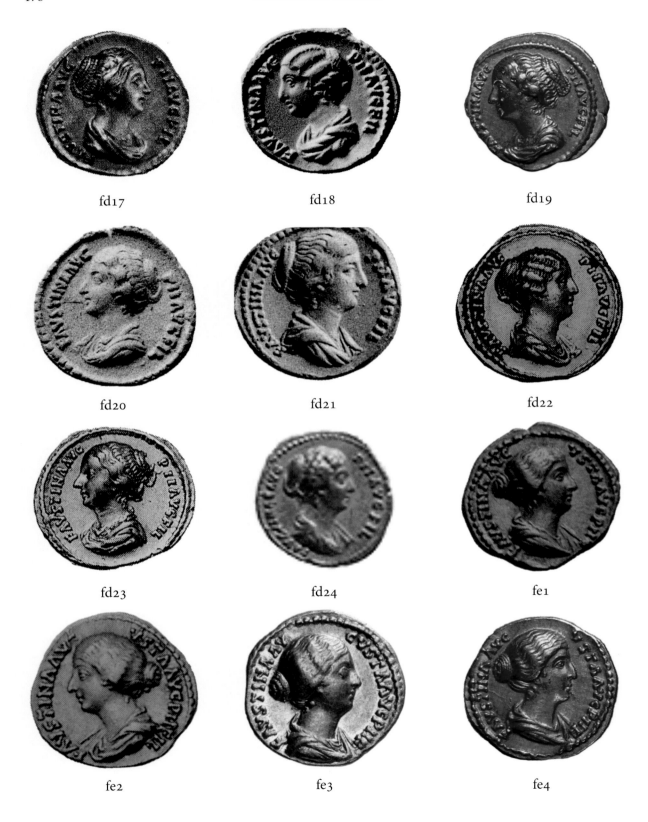

fd17

fd18

fd19

fd20

fd21

fd22

fd23

fd24

fe1

fe2

fe3

fe4

ff1   ff2   ff3

ff4   ff5   ff6

ff7   ff8   ff9

ff10   ff11   ff12

ff13   ff14

ANTONINUS PIUS: REVERSES

AD1   AD2   AD3

AD4   AD5   AD6

AD7   AD8   AD9

AD10   AD11   AD12

AD13   AD14   AD15

AD16   AD17   AD18

AD19   AD20   AD21

AD22   C1   C2

C3   C4   C5

C6   C7   CB1

CB2   CB3   CB4

CB5   CB6   CB7

CB8   CB9   CB10

CB11   CB12   CB13

CB14   CB15   CB16

CB17   CB18   CB19

CB20   CB21   CB23

CB24   CB25   CB26

CB27   CB28   D1

F1   JL1   JL2

JL3   JL4   JS1

JS2   JS3   JS4

JS5   LP1   LP2

LP9   VA1   VA2

VA3   VA4   VA5

LP3   LP4   LP5

LP6   LP7   LP8

VA6

VA7

VA8

VA9

VA10

VA11

VA12

VA13

VA14

VA15

VA16

VA17

VA18   VA19   VA20

VA21   VA22   VA23

VA24   VA25   VA26

VB1   VB2   VB3